**TRANSITION AND
CONTINUITY
IN
THE EDUCATIONAL PROCESS**

Kogan Page Books for Teachers series
Series Editor: Tom Marjoram

Fund-raising for Schools   Gerry Gorman
Making Science Education Relevant   Douglas P Newton
The Place of Physical Education in Schools   Len Almond
Starting to Teach   Anthony D Smith
Teaching Able Children   Tom Marjoram
Towards the National Curriculum   W S Fowler
Transition and Continuity in the Educational Process   Patricia Marshall

TRANSITION AND CONTINUITY IN THE EDUCATIONAL PROCESS

Patricia Marshall

Books for Teachers
Series Editor: Tom Marjoram

KOGAN PAGE

This book is dedicated to
my husband Arthur
without whose help and support
it would never have been!

© Patricia Marshall, 1988

All rights reserved. No reproduction, copy or transmission of this publication may be made without written permission.

No paragraph of this publication may be reproduced, copied or transmitted save with written permission or in accordance with the provisions of the Copyright Act 1956 (as amended), or under the terms of any licence permitting limited copying issued by the Copyright Licensing Agency, 7 Ridgmount Street, London WC1E 7AE.

Any person who does any unauthorised act in relation to this publication may be liable to criminal prosecution and civil claims for damages.

First published in 1988 by
Kogan Page Ltd,
120 Pentonville Road, London N1 9JN

British Library Cataloguing in Publication Data
Marshall, Patricia
   Transition and continuity in the educational process. —
   (Kogan Page books for teachers).
   1. England. Schools. Curriculum. Continuity
   I. Title
   375′.00942

ISBN 1-85091-660-8

Printed and bound in Great Britain by
Biddles Ltd, Guildford

CONTENTS

Acknowledgements 7
Foreword 9
Introduction 11

1
Home to Pre-school Provision 13

Leaving home 13
Parental choices 14
The needs of the child 14
The options in pre-school provision 17
A child's impressions 20
Parents' needs 20
The role of pre-school provision in transition 22
Conclusions concerning pre-school activities 23

2
Home or Pre-school to First School 26

Starting school 26
The physical environment 28
The social environment 28
The curriculum 29
The role of parents in aiding continuity 31
The infant to junior transition 33
Conclusions concerning the first compulsory schooling stage 37

3
From Primary to Secondary Schooling 39

Moving to the big school 39
Children's attitudes 40
Historical background 42
Liaison and curriculum continuity 45
Improvements 49
Records 50
Conclusions concerning this transition 51

4
Through Secondary to 16 and Beyond — 54

    The variety of provision — 54
    Constraints of subject orientation — 55
    Perceived roles of secondary teachers — 56
    Progression through the secondary system — 57
    Current pressures — 59
    Links with post-16 provision — 63
    Careers counselling — 65

5
Particular Issues — 67

    Special needs — 67
    Multicultural teaching — 71
    Community involvement — 73
    Business links — 75

6
What Do We Mean by 'Good Practice?' — 78

    Examples from early years — 78
    'Within school' practices — 84
    Primary/secondary liaison — 85
    Examples of multi-school approaches, federations and consortia — 95
    Careers advice and guidance — 98
    Parental involvement — 100

7
Specific Techniques — 102

    Record-keeping systems — 102
    Assessment and attainment — 105
    Profiling — 111
    Curriculum structure — 117
    Development planning — 119

8
A Summary and Overview of the Current Situation — 120
References — 124

ACKNOWLEDGEMENTS

I would like to express my gratitude to the very many people who have helped in the provision of the material for this book.

Many comments and advice by teachers, parents, pupils and friends have been invaluable in compiling the case studies. Particular thanks are also due to the many authorities who supplied material and have given permission for their practices to be reported.

FOREWORD

The many bridges which children and teenagers have to cross throughout their schooling have long been one of my major concerns. My interest was first aroused in a professional way early on in my career, as a teacher of a fourth-year junior class. In discussion with the children about their fears and anxieties, I was made to reflect on my own childhood experiences. The feelings, still vivid in my memory, of travelling by myself on a school bus at five-years-old from a rural area to a school some four miles away ... it seemed so much further; the transfer from primary school to the large secondary grammar in the county town was initially equally traumatic!

Such experiences and many more as I have become far more deeply involved professionally, encouraged me to undertake a more detailed investigation into the whole 'jungle' of transition and continuity issues. Having viewed the issues from several different standpoints both as consumer and provider through my own childhood and teaching, by having been a headteacher, by providing advice and guidance to teachers and last, but by no means least, as a parent, I believe that I am in a good position to give a balanced view of the various problems and possible solutions.

Throughout the book, I have stressed the role that parents play and I feel very strongly that without their involvement, a critical element is missing in helping children to cross the various bridges that they will encounter.

The study has highlighted how rapidly significant changes are now emerging, both in conventional wisdom, the wider acceptance of the need to tackle continuity issues and in new ideas which are generating innovations in the key issues and problem areas.

Many of the advances in this area are contributing greatly to the professional development of teachers in all areas of education.

The communication between home and school, relationships between children, parents and teachers, still present a particularly relevant and challenging task for all those concerned in the educational process of children and young people; it must be viewed within the context of a commitment to an ideology of equality of opportunity for all. The Hadow Report of 1931 stated:

> It is true, indeed, that the process of education from the age of five to the end of the secondary stage, should be envisaged as a coherent whole. That there should be no sharp divide between infant, junior, and post primary stages, and that the transition from any one stage to the succeeding stage should be as smooth and gradual as possible.

There is really very little that is new!

A tearful five-year-old on his third day of conscription into the reception class declared,

'I DIDN'T WANT TO JOIN ANYWAY.'

Again a Hadow Report, this time from 1926, stated:

> Transplanted to new ground and set in a new environment, which should be adjusted, as far as possible, to the interests and abilities of each range and variety, we believe that they will thrive to a new height and attain sturdier fibre.

It really is about time we got to grips with some of the more obvious problems. Many of them do not require complex solutions, merely the enthusiasm and will!

Patricia Marshall
May 1988

INTRODUCTION

This book aims to demonstrate how children fare in the transitions they must make from one phase of their education to another between the ages of 3 and 16 years.

Much has been written, separately, about the different stages of education they go through, but it is important to see how each phase fits into the entirety of the whole process, and to understand the consequences of one stage on another. The intention of this book is to give insight into the wide range of discontinuities that children can be subjected to, depending on what individual experiences they undergo, from home through to leaving the full-time educational system, so that the teacher can take suitable action to avoid the identifiable pitfalls.

The main body of the book is in four parts corresponding to the four major 'bridges of transition in compulsory education':

a) The first covers the stage from home through to the various forms of pre-school provision, whatever that might be, bearing in mind the tremendous range of disparity between what is on offer, (Chapter 1).
b) The second part looks at the problems encountered on entering the first stage of compulsory education, focusing particularly on curriculum continuity between infant and junior departments, (Chapter 2).
c) The third part is devoted to 'moving to the big school'; the primary to secondary bridge of transition, (Chapter 3).
d) The fourth is an examination of the various avenues through secondary education and, more briefly, from the age of 16 onward, (Chapter 4).

It is clear that there should be carefully defined goals for all children and a unity of purpose throughout the 3–16 educational span according to individual needs. As a consequence of the wide diversity of provision for a child's schooling, not only in the pre-school phase, but in sizes, types and social environments of primary, middle and secondary schools, there is a need for a far greater continuity in what is offered to pupils of all ages. The curricular differences due to the social, political, administrative, economic and philosophical differences which prevail are numerous. The following chapters attempt to explore the issues which give rise to these differences and examine what could and is being done at this time. The only certainty is that the changes cannot take place overnight since they involve changing attitudes and beliefs in many cases. Because of this it is probably the individual teachers and heads who can have the biggest effect on improving transition and continuity, not just within their own spheres of influence but also in the schools they receive pupils from or send them to.

Today with the emphasis on more and more accountability, it is even more important that we review what continuity of experiences is being offered to children. There is need continually to look for ways to improve and integrate the learning processes so that all children have as smooth a path through the educational system as is feasible.

The book also attempts to look at some specific issues that are increasingly needing careful attention, such as special needs, multicultural teaching situations and records and assessment, but specifically in the *context of transition and continuity*. There are also many examples of good practice embedded within the text but particular examples are documented in more detail in order to provide the practitioner with some 'starter ideas' which could be extrapolated to local situations. The information used has been collected from a wide diversity of sources, the majority of which are the LEAs in the UK who have been very helpful in supplying information on their activities.

The book is mainly aimed at both newcomers to the profession and experienced practitioners. Because of the current emphasis on transition and continuity, it will be particularly useful to headteachers, those involved in in-service training, governors and advisory bodies.

CHAPTER 1
HOME TO PRE-SCHOOL PROVISION

'Leaving home'

Continuity in a young child's life is very important. Therefore, in terms of leaving home for the first time, we should question how much awareness there is in regard to his or her needs and whether enough thought is given to making this transition as smooth and non-threatening as possible. The experiences the child undergoes in this early period will set the precedents for the rest of his or her school experiences.

The Council of Europe's Declaration (1979), after ten years of study of the care and education of children at the pre-school stage, emphasized the need for continuity of experience both within the child's home and community and between the different parts of the organizations concerned with care and education.

> ... this declaration is a serious challenge to us to engage in further study of what experiences mean to young children in relation to continuity and discontinuity and what beneficial rather than harmful experiences can be provided. (Margaret Roberts, 1981)

This quotation has been given in full because of the weight it gives to the argument for the need for a better understanding of the transition process.

As awareness grows regarding how crucial the early years of a child's life are to the influence they are to have on that child's later learning, far greater attention must be paid to the experiences and guidance offered to children at each stage of their development. Sylva and Lunt (1982) say of the lasting effects of pre-school education, 'for the first time we have sound evidence from American studies that early intervention can have a powerful influence on a child's prospects'. Equal importance needs to be paid to helping the child to cross the transitional bridge safely and securely in order to make the progress through the educational processes as smooth as possible. It is also important that we bear in mind that bridges are two-way thoroughfares; there is a constant need to refer back to the experiences which came before, in order that secure links can be made with what is found on the other side of the 'bridge'! We must look 'from home to pre-school, but in terms of a continual and changing interplay of effects between the child's, experiences in the pre-school and the home environment' (Blatchford *et al*, 1982).

Parental choices

Having provided evidence for the need to examine the transition question, it is now time to explore the variety of options available to parents in providing for their children's needs outside the home environment. This issue will be examined from the three different viewpoints of the child, the parents and the pre-school care providers.

As parents have many different motives for seeking assistance in caring for their children outside the home, this chapter examines the various transitions that children might make from home to child-minders, to play groups, to day nurseries, to nursery schools and to nursery classes. Bearing in mind the needs of the parents, child and receiving organizers, the plan is to investigate how much preparation is made, given and received, in order that the transition is a smooth and successful process. Links will be made between theory and practice, to illustrate where there are gaps, so that ways can be suggested in which these might be overcome.

The needs of the child

The logical place to begin this study is with the child and the parents.

No child has ever asked to be born; no child has had the chance to choose their natural parents. It is obvious, but so often ignored by those primarily concerned with the economics and 'macro-objectives' of the educational systems, that parents and the home environment can have dramatic and sometimes disturbing effects on a child's whole life. The current publicity, rightly given to child abuse, has brought this into stark relief.

It is impossible within the context of this study to classify individual children and the homes in which they are brought up.

What we can do, is generalize about the type of home experiences the child might have before the first venture outside the home and this is often, indeed, the best that can be done in so many areas affecting educational processes, as teachers rarely get the opportunity to visit pupils' homes. Ways must be found to assess each child's particular needs. One possibility is to spend time getting to know each child and the parents well so that there is complete trust resulting in openness, sincerity and honesty providing a sound understanding of the child and the home environment. Not only does this require a highly developed set of social skills on behalf of the teacher, but with all the other pressures on teachers' time, both external and internal, this ideal can rarely be achieved in full.

It is a well established fact that a child's early years are the major growth period for language, conceptual and social development. The work of Bloom on intelligence concludes that '50 per cent of the variance in intelligence at 17 years of age is determined by the age of four years and 80 per cent by the age of eight' (Bloom, 1964, p 88). It is inevitable that a secure and caring home background, which is rich in experiences, is highly influential in this. For more theoretical background there is little need to look further than Piaget for his views on imaginative thought, in all its facets, as the fundamental basis of continuity in the development of mental attributes. His concept of 'assimilation' and 'accommodation', working in conjunction with equilibration, provides an understanding of how children adapt to change. Another theory he put forward stated that a child uses past experiences to cope with new experiences and this provides much of the basis for present educational practices.

It is during the years up to five that 'a child is developing most rapidly and is learning more than at any time in his life' (Sylva and Lunt, 1982). Ideally it is within the security of a sheltered home background that the infant begins to learn appropriate life skills.

There are strong views which suggest that the child's early years are best spent entirely with the mother. The work of John Bowlby (1971) supports this idea and his report to the World Health Organisation in 1953 argued that it is essential for the child's normal social and intellectual development. However, more recent research has shown that a child's relationships with other adults and siblings had previously been undervalued (Blatchford, 1979). Many mothers would agree with Bowlby that they are the best people to bring up their children in the pre-school years and, of course, can make a very good job of it. These mothers choose not to involve outside agencies, but, for many, motherhood does not give them sufficient self-fulfilment and for a variety of reasons these mothers seek the help of outside agencies in caring for their young. Yet again, other social and economic pressures very often cause mothers to have to combine bringing up their children with other work, whether it be full or part time. Most mothers need and benefit from some form of break from their small and demanding infant and, sometimes, they will need help in meeting some educational or developmental needs which are outside their capability or capacity. In either case they frequently seek some kind of 'nursery provision'.

Unfortunately, there are many children who lack a secure or caring family background and this seems to be an increasing fact in our present society across all the socio-economic scales. It is self-evident that good family relationships are a sound basis for the well-being of children; the failure of adults to establish lasting relationships, whatever the reason, is likely to have a detrimental effect on the children brought up in such homes. Long-term unemployment with little prospect of work leads to tension, stress and sometimes the destruction of many relationships, resulting in a further increase and emotional pressure on one-parent families. Together with the relative ease with which divorces and remarriages can be obtained, these factors appear to be some of the causes leading to children showing abnormal behaviour patterns.

Help is needed for these children and it is often via the advice of the 'caring' agencies such as the Department of Health and Social Security (DHSS) that parents seek and obtain pre-school care and educational requirements outside the home.

Before moving on to examine the variety of provision that may be available, it is important to reiterate that 'good family relationships minimise the risk of problems arising in the child's well being and development, the mothers role being the key' (Bowlby 1971).

Parents, then, play an important role in the education of their children and the talents they can develop. An excellent example of this is the involvement of the parents in the 'Children's Palaces' concept in China, which will be discussed further in Chapter 6.

To return to the analogy of a two-way bridge for transition, it is relevant that the experiences the child has gained in the home environment are carefully linked to the chosen pre-school approach so that smooth adjustment can be made.

The options in pre-school provision

Four major options are now described. Since they are so diverse, it has not been practicable to classify the various other 'care' arrangements made either privately by individual parents (eg relations or neighbours) or work place facilities (eg creches). Regrettably, the pre-school opportunities which are now described vary in quality and also provision varies enormously with where you happen to live.

CHILD-MINDING

This is the practice whereby women, usually in their own homes, look after other people's children and for which they are paid. This may be for a whole or part day arrangement. There has recently been a considerable increase in this type of provision for reasons mentioned previously. As many child-minders are not registered it is difficult to obtain statistics for the number of children being cared for in this way.

The Law requires that if a person is paid to look after children for more that two hours per day, in the privacy of their own home, they should register themselves with the local authority. The social services departments of local authorities are supposed to inspect the suitability of child-minders before they can become registered, which for some could be a disincentive to register. If there are few incentives to do so, unregistered child-minders could invite suspicion, even though they might provide a perfectly competent service. The DHSS and the social services use registered child-minders for those children brought into care and considered to be at risk.

Little is known about the quality of care provided by child-minders, but Mayell and Petrie (1977) gained some insight when they carried out a study which concentrated on children under two years of age. They compared the child's relationship with the mother to that of the child-minder and found that, far from 'being like home', many children did not interact with the child-minder and often showed signs of being subdued and inhibited. The Oxford Pre-school Research Project (Bruner *et al*, 1980) confirmed this, finding that two-thirds of the children observed were detached and did not communicate with their child-minders. This seems to indicate that there is a lack of attention paid to smoothing the passage from one environment to the other. Because it is difficult to monitor the quality of care in this area, it is not easy to see a pattern of familiarization that a child might experience.

Indeed it is difficult to see how adequate quality standards can be set and maintained across this type of provision, without setting up large and costly inspectorate systems.

The provision is far better managed when the parents show concern and are happy with the transition. This usually results in pre-visits, with the mother or father staying for a while and the child-minder initially visiting the child at his or her home. Toys and treasured objects are taken and left with the child-minder.

Parents may find it difficult to select the right person for their child if there are few choices available, and payment may vary considerably with the quality of provision. All too often a child-minder is more concerned with such things as order, routine, cleanliness etc, than with developing similar natural interactions a child might experience with his or her mother. To build up a relationship with each child, particularly if there are three or four more children in the home, is not an easy task for the child-minder. This leads us to believe that a child could miss out on a lot of learning which would normally have taken place in the child's own home. Tizard and Hughes (1984) demonstrated the 'home to be a very powerful learning environment'.

Bad experiences could be avoided if child-minding were to come under some kind of 'watchdog' such as an 'Early Learning Council'. Children fare much better where child-minders involve themselves with other groups and organizations such as 'Mothers and Toddlers' or the British Association for Early Childhood Education and also make visits outside their own community.

Playgroups

These were introduced in 1960 and were conceived on the lines of a 'do-it-yourself' nursery system with the major emphasis on play activities. According to Bruner (1975), playgroups then catered for over half-a-million children under five years of age. Usually children attend for two to three sessions a week for which a fee is charged. There are approximately 20 children at any one session and, as Crowe (1973) says,

> ... all that can be taken for granted is that the premises and the playgroup leader have been passed as satisfying the criteria of the DHSS, that the ratio of children to adults has been officially limited and that the group has not been allowed to start unless the leader was suitably qualified to satisfy the Pre-School Playgroups Association.

As staff are frequently mothers of children who also attend, their own children's transition should be reasonably smooth; other children may still find the break traumatic so 'Mum' is usually encouraged to stay and therefore ease the child into the new situation. The physical environment and sharing an adult may take some adjusting to, as well as aspects of furthering the child's social and emotional development. Although these are better controlled, there is still considerable variation in the quality of provision and much depends on the organizational skills of the leader.

Day nurseries
These are financed by the DHSS with the emphasis on care because they primarily exist to care for children while parents work full time. Unlike the other nurseries, they take babies from as young as a few weeks' old. Hours are generally between 7.00 am and 6.00 pm and priority is generally given to children who are 'at risk'.

In many ways these day nurseries provide a valuable service, and are managed by properly trained staff who provide many experiences which these children would otherwise be denied. This must contribute considerably to their development and may well compensate for some of the problems that arise in the home environment due to the child's frequent full-day absences.

Parents are encouraged to become involved and many staff work hard to foster home and nursery links; the very nature of the domestic backgrounds of many of their charges can make such opportunities very limited, however.

Nursery schools and classes
These are maintained and supported by the Local Education Authorities and children attend, usually part time, for part of every weekday in the normal term times. The major difference between nursery schools and classes is that the former are entities in their own right, whereas the latter are usually part of an infant or primary school. The staff comprise professionally trained teachers and NNEB qualified nurses. Historically the nursery concept has been fostered by educationalists such as Froebel, Isaacs, the McMillans, Montessori, etc (Curtis, 1986). The educational aims are concerned with improving the child's social, intellectual and physical skills through a carefully integrated curriculum which is planned and implemented by professionals.

A pattern of pre-school visits plus a home visit by a member of staff is not unusual and is certainly the practice within many LEAs and also in many nursery units. Parents are seen to be crucial to the ease of this transition. To quote a head of a highly acclaimed nursery school, 'I insist that all parents become involved, so that we get to know each other fully, because only in that way can we get to know what is best for their child.' Many opportunities are created in order that there should be complete understanding of the child's needs.

A child's impressions

In looking at the needs and feelings of a child leaving the security of home for the first time, the question which needs to be asked is, 'So what does all this mean to the child?' Feelings will vary enormously according to home experiences and how independent the mother has encouraged her child to become. The physical environment will undoubtedly become enlarged, especially when moving to the nursery or play group, and will seem strange and somewhat insecure to all but a very few.

If adults were occasionally to get down to the child's eye level from time to time, they might begin to get a better understanding of the feelings the child is likely to experience. The fact that the child is likely to be sharing the adult's attention with other children can prove frustrating and needs patient understanding. Noise levels may be distressing at first and situations necessary for group organization will be strange. Indeed, times for eating and drinking will be governed and the situation of the toilet, requiring the child to cope alone, will be less distressing for the child who has had some training. Standards at home often differ greatly and the language used at school may be quite strange depending on the home environment, almost a 'book' language to some. Little things that the child takes for granted at home will differ – for example, where things are kept. Activities allowed in one environment may be unacceptable in another, such as painting, playing with water, etc . . . the list can seem endless to the child.

Parents' needs

In order that parents can play their essential part in smooth transition and in promoting continuity, they are likely to need help in understanding the significance of the processes involved. Allowing another person or group to join them in caring for their child can often lead to a feeling of relinquishing their authority and autonomy and, sometimes, of inadequacy.

In the case of child-minding or day nurseries, mothers can have guilt feelings: putting the 'need to work' or their own 'self-interests' before the needs of their children. Many of these guilt feelings can be eased by the careful choice of child-minder together with visits, each way, to establish confidence that the parent is taking the best available action. Similar emotions prevail with day nurseries, and these are also significantly eased if the child is sufficiently familiar with the new environment; this again is best achieved by adequate preparation.

Usually a child reaches a certain age before leaving his or her mother for a group situation. The playgroup or nursery, being the most common, almost invariably encourage the parents to become involved in participating with their children; this can only lessen the sense of 'breaking away from home'. The nursery school and such classes are often seen by parents as the first rung of the conventional educational ladder and the first step their child makes towards independence from home. 'The process of giving up the child to the educational system is also likely to induce or confirm parents' feeling of inadequacy' (Tizard *et al*, 1981). This is the time for the nursery to capitalize on the 'parental involvement' strongly advocated in the Plowden Report (1967); it is while their children are at this stage that parents are most likely to be involved in school, if only to bring and fetch them. Too often in the past, not enough has been done to make parents aware that they are not handing their children over to the experts to be properly educated, but that without their cooperation and interest children will be unable to take advantage of the opportunities that are newly available. Parents need to know how much the nursery or playgroup value their concerns in order that the first steps across the bridge between home and education will be as smooth and anxiety-free as possible. This is endorsed by the recommendation of Plowden who said that, 'parental involvement encouraged at this stage will be seed well sown, for it will flourish throughout the child's education; without this strong bond schools cannot achieve the best results for their charges on behalf of the parents.'

The role of pre-school provision in transition

Many schools strive hard to get and keep parents participating, whether on an individual basis or by involving them in school or social activities. Possibly the first contact with the child and parent is when they arrive to put the child's name down for admission. This is the time to show parents a warm welcome; for giving them a tour of the establishment, introducing them to everyone and providing information which they might find helpful. Some parents may feel shy or uncomfortable with professional people, so great care must be taken to make them feel at ease and to provide a climate in which they feel they can ask questions or express their misgivings. This transition can be even more daunting in a multiethnic or multicultural environment, for child, parent and staff, in nurseries or playgroups where language difficulties prove a problem. However, if the staff are aware of this situation beforehand, they may be able to ensure that the services of an interpreter (usually one of the mothers in the group) are available and that translations of notices and information are readily available.

Sometimes a pre-school club is formed for mothers and toddlers, if space is available. The nursery network in Newcastle particularly favours this idea and has produced some useful video tapes which could be helpful to other areas. The child and his or her mother are invited to join in various social activities prior to entry and this is a valuable aid to transition, because not only are the child and mother getting to know the school, but also the teaching staff are able to build up a profile of the child by seeing him or her with his or her parents. A further way this concept can be aided is by the teacher visiting the child at home. As research (Tizard *et al*, 1981) has shown, many parents do find school intimidating but in their own home they can feel more relaxed and in control when asking questions or expressing opinions. Providing the home visit is seen as a way of getting to know each other by building up a friendship between child, parent and teacher, much can be gained. Unfortunately, this is not always possible for a variety of reasons, often logistical. However, in rural areas, parents may feel or actually be more isolated, and the home visit can be a very useful aid in ensuring continuity of experience between home and school.

It is important to give priority and time to talking with parents about school routines and how best to prepare the child for these. Often headteachers and their staff devote considerable time and effort to getting parents together and talking about the importance of language in child development. The nursery prospectus is introduced, perhaps when discussing aims and educational issues such as the value of play, etc. Involving established parents to talk with new parents during a social activity, is a particularly useful way to allay some anxieties. If the way has been sufficiently well paved, then settling into the new environment should be a smooth transition. Mothers are encouraged to stay until their child has settled and as the start of term is often staggered to accommodate a few children at a time, more attention can be devoted to the new arrivals. If a child is unhappy and is inclined to cling to the mother, she can often feel embarrassed so must be helped to ease herself gradually away, perhaps by involving herself with a group of children. As one headteacher has said, 'it is so important that a mother tells her child when she leaves that she will return at a certain time and to make sure that she does and is prompt'. Usually the child settles when the mother has departed, but it is good practice, where possible, to telephone the mother at home to provide her with reassurance, particularly if the situation has been especially traumatic or difficult. In order to keep in close contact with parents, even when their children are well settled, there is a need to keep various activities going both in and out of school time. Perhaps by arranging some form of parent-teacher activities, remembering that working parents cannot manage day-time meetings and baby sitters may need to be specially booked for evening meetings.

The more children are able to see parents and teachers working together the more they benefit from the friendship and understanding which inevitably tends to develop.

Conclusions concerning pre-school activities

It is evident that there is a large and, indeed, fast growing demand for nursery and other forms of pre-school provision. There is, therefore, a need to prepare for increased provision as well as improving present practices for effective transition and continuity within the educational system. In view of this there is much happening already, but overall there is considerable room for improvement. This can be summarized by stressing the need for more awareness, communication and, by no means least, information to be exchanged between parents and staff at pre-school centres.

To become aware of the needs of young children in crossing the first bridge of their educational journey, as teachers, parents and as a community, more channels of communication along which information can flow freely, need to be established. By carefully using government funding, in some areas provision for the under-fives is coming together under one umbrella and the regular meeting of the various agencies now ensures better communication on issues of mutual concern. Parents are beginning to have earlier access to information on pre-school activities via health visitors and teacher counsellors. Certainly, an ever increasing number of children with special needs are being identified at far earlier stages than in the past as a result of such co-operation.

An area where there could be more benefit to the child is the encouragement of greater communication between playgroups and the nursery schools and classes. Many children are attending both at some time, so one should undoubtedly complement the other, at least within a particular locality, by sharing ideas and activities and by exchanging some recorded information whether in writing or verbally. Ideally, a way of easing the transition from one form of provision to another would be by the formation of a General Early Years Council (Cleave *et al*, 1982).

The report *Experimental Liaison Groups in Early Education* (Bate *et al*, 1982) was influential in groups being established in different areas of the country jointly under the local education authorities and social services. Members included representatives of first, infant and primary schools together with other surrounding forms of pre-school provision. These groups proved a very useful way of starting a movement towards co-ordinating services for the young children in a given area. The growth of this concept is bound to enhance ways of smoothing transition and providing some form of continuity. This could only accelerate with greater government recognition.

Much more could be done through the better provision of in-service courses for all who are connected with pre-school provision. The more that is understood, the more likely that the transition from one stage of learning to another will be painless and enjoyable for all – not just the child! If we accept that new environments help people to develop and grow, then 'discontinuity in the form of a new and stimulating experience within a secure framework is an excellent way of extending the child's learning and understanding . . . ' (Curtis, 1986).

Parents benefit as well as their children if more information is available on how they should play their part in helping their children to cross this bridge of transition from home to pre-school. It is vital, however, that this information is in a form which is acceptable to, and suitable for, the parent, rather than produced for the teaching professional and steeped in educational 'jargon'.

The one area that does need greater attention and seems to lack adequate quality control, is that of child-minding. Registration should be a much more positive activity and deserves better follow-up. So little sanction seems to be exerted on failure to register; either the penalties need to be more of a deterrent or there should be very clear benefits, such as tax or special purchase concessions. It is difficult, however, to envisage what can be done to improve the situation without turning the activity into a bureaucratic nightmare. Perhaps the real solution is to increase the other forms of provision, thus the need for child-minders would become less and less, except in the care of babies.

Much of this chapter is closely related to entry into the infant school, which is the subject of the next chapter of this book.

Finally, to complete this crossing from home to pre-school, the following quotation is very appropriate:

> When a seedling is transplanted from one place to another, the transplantation may be a stimulus or a shock. The careful gardener seeks to minimise the shock so that the plant is re-established as quickly as possible. Similarly, for the child moving from one form of provision to another, a smooth transition requires that the change is sufficient to be stimulating, but not so drastic as to cause shock. (Cleave *et al*, 1982, p 145)

CHAPTER 2
HOME OR PRE-SCHOOL TO FIRST SCHOOLS

Starting school

This chapter covers the first stage of compulsory education and the transition made between infant and junior departments. Much has already been written concerning the first entry of children into school infant classes but relatively little on the latter. The emphasis in these critical stages will be on the discontinuities experienced by the child and the vital role of parents in transitional processes. Curriculum will be given greater attention when the specific transfer to junior from infant school is examined. To link this with the first bridge it is essential to return to a further quotation from the Council of Europe Survey (1977), which proposes that:

> Whatever the age of compulsory schooling in member countries – the years 3-8 should be seen as a continuum and there should be no break in curriculum or methods between pre-school provision and early stages of primary schooling.

Why is it so important to be concerned about smoothing the pathway from one stage of education to another? Not so long ago this process was not even considered and children 'coped' or at least appeared to do so. Inevitably, there will always be some children who will take the first steps unaided and with a degree of confidence, and who will benefit from the experience. This is very much dependent however, on the attitudes of their parents and the preparation they have received before the start of their formal schooling.

Starting school is a big step, certainly bigger for those children who go straight from home as opposed to coming from some form of pre-school provision. Unfortunately, an increasing number of children from unstable or uncaring home situations have inadequate preparation, particularly from their parents, and these children will inevitably have a difficult start to their education.

Much research over recent years by child psychologists, such as Bruner (1960), Piaget and Inhelder (1969) and Bloom (1964), has indicated that the experiences formed in the early years and the importance of continuity in the child's learning are crucial to later development. Although the evidence is not conclusive, research in the USA in the 1970s does give some weight to the notion that we need to give a much higher priority to smoothing the transition between the different phases of the educational processes, so that children will benefit and not be hindered by the poor experiences they can have if inadequately prepared.

Unfortunately, according to other research (Cleave *et al*, 1982) vertical discontinuity existed for many children transferring from home and pre-school provision to the first phase of compulsory schooling. It is also sad to note, and this is borne out both by my personal experience and by various authorities (for example, Bennett *et al*, 1984), that this vertical discontinuity is also quite common within schools, as well as existing between different stages of schooling.

Change is inevitable throughout life and providing that it is a gradual process and sufficient preparation is given in order to eliminate or at least to minimize the impact of potential discontinuities, then such changes can become stimulating and valuable learning experiences. This is put very succinctly by Plowden (para 427) 1967:

> Children, like adults, enjoy and are stimulated by novelty and change. The first day at school, the transfer to the "big" school are landmarks in the process of growing up. Even when children are apprehensive, they look forward to change, but, if change is to stimulate and not to dishearten, it must be carefully prepared and not be too sudden . . .

This process clearly requires a great deal of liaison and understanding between pre-school educators and teachers in the infant sector. In this and other situations the key people are the parents and their role will be discussed in detail later. First, it is important to examine some of the areas which can give rise to discontinuities when a child starts compulsory schooling. Inevitably, there will be overlap between the problems described in this and the previous chapter and, to a lesser extent, the subsequent chapters.

The physical environment

Any change in our physical surroundings is bound to have a significant influence on how we react, whether as children or adults. Cleave *et al* (1982) identified three features critical for children, whatever their previous experience:

a) The scale and size of the building and its contents.
b) The range and extent of their territory and the siting of facilities such as play areas, toilets, etc.
c) Organizational constraints in moving around the territory and within their 'base'.

Certainly, children coming straight from home are more overwhelmed by the sheer scale of the building than those children who have had previous experience of group situations. Children from nursery and playgroups, although more used to large spaces, often find the arrangment of furniture and play equipment very different and more restricting on movement and activities (Curtis, 1986). Even as adults, we feel more at ease if we know the geographical layout of facilities and what we are free to use. Organizational limitations will also have their effect on children, whether they come straight from home or a pre-school setting, in terms of their freedom of movement and their choice of whether or not to become involved in an activity. To go into more detail here would duplicate the studies of Cleave *et al* (1982) Blatchford *et al* (1982) and Curtis (1986). It is worth reiterating their general point, though, that familiarity provides children with security and confidence in their surroundings and much preparation has to take place to enable children to feel at ease when moving from one environment to another.

The social environment

Many children straight from home may find that being part of a larger group is difficult to cope with, whereas others will be fairly confident – this will depend very much on their personality and previous experiences. All children are affected by the adult to child ratio when starting school. At home some children may have an adult's undivided attention or at most have to share with one or two siblings.

Even in playgroups and nursery settings there are usually many adults 'on tap'. The proportion of adults in the infant class setting is very much reduced, which necessitates a child being immediately more self-contained and able to cope for him or herself. For example, there is a sense of achievement if the child can undress and dress him or herself for PE and at playtimes, rather than having to wait for assistance from a teacher who has 25 or more other infants to look after.

Getting used to a planned timetable, rather than having comparative freedom of choice, is inhibiting and the findings in the study of Cleave *et al* (1982) produced very interesting data. For example, the study found that two-thirds of the children's time in the infant class was spent in carrying out teacher-directed activities. My own experience correlates with Cleave's observation that teaching styles and individual ideologies vary tremendously, both in pre-school and primary education; what is expected of children in the reception classes in schools can also vary enormously. It is clear that where there is more communication and consistency of routines between all concerned, the children will experience less discontinuity and trauma.

The curriculum

Children straight from home will find most of the daily activities completely new, unless their parents have taken great interest and spent considerable time in preparing them for the transition; they are likely to have different patterns of expectation and adjustment to nursery-experienced children. The freedom to choose activities is often restricted by the different aims of the teachers and the siting and range of equipment in the infant classroom. Free choice is allowed usually only after the more 'formal' work has been completed.

Indeed, some of the recent pressures to move towards greater accountability have resulted in more teachers over-stressing the basic skills at a very early age, thus allowing too little time for the more creative aspects of the curriculum. These were findings common to two DES reports, *Education 5–9* (1982) and *The Primary Report* (1978). The lack of awareness on the part of many parents of their role in encouraging creativity and enabling the child to capitalize on basic skills is difficult to overcome. This problem could well grow if parents are given too much authority to influence the school curriculum. (The 1986 Education Act (No. 2) gives more representation to parents on Governing Bodies.)

Areas of expectation, which may differ considerably between home to school and pre-school to school, are likely to be greater in behaviour and language. What is acceptable in one situation is often totally unacceptable in another – this, of course, is not confined to children! Teachers need to be aware of just how much family values, discipline and morality can differ from those expected in school, whether these originate from the parents themselves, various bodies within the community or from the pressures of society at large. Consistency is highly desirable between all those involved – conflict very often results when children encounter unexpected or unexplained differences. Fortunately for us, children are very adaptable and are quick to learn that certain behaviours are acceptable in one setting and not acceptable in others. It helps considerably if adults, both at school and at home, are consistent in their examples, thus ensuring that this essential 'life-skill' learning takes place.

Language also comes into this behaviour pattern. For some children entering school for the first time the language base can often be very different and difficult to comprehend – this can apply even to articulate children. Deprived children, or children from an environment where English may not be the first or only language used, may have considerable problems. Taking in information and carrying out instructions can be confusing at first and expressing views and thoughts may be difficult – and even more so for children with limited linguistic ability. Of all the areas where continuity is critical language must, surely, rank as one of the highest priorities. Even the most articulate children are bound to find some discontinuity because our whole language structure is so complex. Teachers and pre-school educators need to devote much more time and attention to this aspect, for its continuity is essential if children are to make satisfactory and smooth progress. This applies not only to children transferring from one institution to another, but also between one class and another within a school. Much research in this area has been carried out by Tizard and Hughes (1984) and Wells (1985).

When viewing the curriculum as a whole in order to minimize discontinuities, it can be seen that the philosophies and ideologies of both those who run pre-school activities and those in infant teaching need to have a far greater degree of 'match'. Each will need to relinquish some of their autonomy and independence of attitude. The survey carried out by the British Association for Early Childhood Education in 1984 into the needs of a five-year-old in infant classes emphasized just that point.

There needs to be a much clearer definition of what each stage of education aims to provide and enable the child to accomplish in all aspects of the curriculum.

The role of parents in aiding continuity

As highlighted earlier, parents are or should be the main supporting arch in the bridge of transition at whatever stage of education is being examined. If parents are such a powerful source of continuity then both parents and teachers should constantly seek opportunities to explore their mutual understanding of each other's 'worlds'. The onus, however, is on the teacher to start this process, being the 'professional' who understands the potential for misinterpretation which can arise.

In the previous section reference was made to the need for the educators to have a better understanding of the early stages of education and what each stage sets out to achieve. Clearly, parents also need to comprehend what each of these stages is setting out to achieve for their child; many do not and are often not encouraged to appreciate the value of nursery and pre-school education (as was expressed so clearly by Tizard *et al*, 1981). There is a need to promote this benefit more. Quite often the active involvement of some parents is the only link between playgroups, nursery schools and infant class.

When talking with nursery and infant teachers about their pupils' previous experiences, it is not surprising to find that they have little knowledge of whether the children have been to playgroups nor do they really know what experiences the children have had before coming into their charge. Parents need to be considered more when professionals are discussing and planning for their child's transition, particularly at primary levels.

Tizard and Hughes (1984) found that the learning which goes on at home was likely to be significantly different to that at school and the following quotation is very appropriate:

> It is time to shift the emphasis from what parents should learn from professionals towards what professionals can learn from studying parents and children at home.

We can but be sceptical about how far professionals are truly prepared to come along this path, whatever their overt declarations!

Too often parents feel excluded from their child's education. A great deal of misunderstanding and suspicion could be avoided by more involvement with parents, particularly in record compilation and transfer. Although it is the practice of some schools not to pass on detailed records in the belief that the child can start again with a 'clean sheet', surely there is a far greater need to be aware of what has occurred before in order effectively to plan what should come next. Piaget's (1961) pyramidal nature of learning and Bruner's (1960) spiral curriculum together with De Witt's (1977) home and community examples are just a few of the eminent psychologists who support this approach.

It is all very well to identify the areas of need for parental involvement in continuity, but when this is feasible there still remain some immense difficulties in actually securing this involvement. Many of these difficulties are vested in the variety of pre-school facilities available, the dispersion of the catchment area and the sheer time required. Where one pre-school feeds many infant classes, or where a school receives from many pre-schools, it is often impossible to involve all concerned in a full transition programme (this problem recurs with even more significance in the primary to secondary bridge).

There is nothing new in this problem. In 1977 a research project was established to look into transition and continuity in early education for the three-to-eight-years age group as was mentioned in Chapter 1 (Bate *et al*, 1982). This explored the activities of liaison groups which were comprised of staff in the schools and all forms of pre-school provision in the area, together with some parents and local health visitors. Their brief was threefold:

a) To consider what *they* saw as continuity in the early years as related to their own environment;
b) To identify any problems there may be within the pre-school provision and from pre-school to the first school;
c) to make recommendations for ensuring smooth transition and continuity in the early years.

Interestingly, the Cleave (1982) project found that 'there was a marked tendency for non-professionals to view the expertise of teachers as a barrier to communication'. This has implications for liaison which could, perhaps, play an important role in preparing teachers and nursery nurses to work effectively with other adults concerned with the care and education of the young. This is my own experience and applies not only to non-professionals but also, particularly, to parents as illustrated by Watt (1985) in his work on *The Role of Parents in the Continuity of Children's Education*. Teachers need to be helped in order to explain themselves in a context and language that are meaningful and non-threatening to parents. This must be a fruitful area on which to focus in-service education, especially at local level, and could well provide a positive benefit; there is no real reason why parents and governors should not come together and become involved in such training activities.

The infant to junior transition

Much of what has been said concerning the pre-school to infant transition applies to the subsequent primary stages, particularly those references to the lack of liaison and communication between professionals. For this reason the emphasis in this section will be on record keeping and curriculum issues associated with the infant to junior stage. Transfer at the end of the child's infant education may be within the same school or to another junior school, often on the same campus.

CONTINUITY

Continuity in a combined junior and infant school is bound to be smoother when it comes to the physical and organizational aspects, but contrary to expectations that the same applies in regard to curriculum, this is frequently not the case (Bennett *et al*, 1984).

Where children actually move from one school to another, say at the age of seven years or eight to nine years depending on Local Authority provisions, then of course there will be a certain level of discontinuity in the physical and organizational routines to which the children will need to adapt to. This is, however, obvious and therefore much more likely to be recognized as a potential problem which has to be solved.

In a junior mixed infant (JMI) school the boundaries are seldom seen as requiring special attention, but at least we should expect greater flexbility. *The Primary Report* (DES, 1978) gave some evidence that it was usual for some inter-school visiting to take place prior to transfers but suggested that much more should be done.

Looking at the curriculum continuity, the report also remarked that: 'the importance of continuity in the curriculum of schools was largely overlooked'.

Dean (1985) notes this as an important observation, yet no further comments or recommendations were made in the report. However, it did go on to say that most schools give continuity priority to language and mathematics as a consequence of the heavy emphasis on, and nature of, the structure and sequence of learning needed in those areas. In thematic studies, for instance, few schools or teachers seemed to have an overall plan or structured approach. Topic frequently follows topic in a fairly haphazard way. Some topics may be repeated in subsequent classes or others inadvertently omitted. Phrases and words like 'fragmented', 'random', 'repetition', and 'lack of regular planning' were often used in *The Primary Report* to describe the teaching of subjects such as history, geography and social studies.

In order that children do not get bored and waste their time repeating work, much more attention needs to be given to the experiences children bring with them from their previous classes, home and community. Walkerdine (1982) found that teachers often underestimated this when, in mathematics, children are asked to do 'shopping sums' with values completely unrelated to those used in their own shopping perceptions; many other examples could be given. The entire staff of a school needs to be involved in the formulation of curriculum policies and in determining the means by which these are integrated and implemented. In a JMI school it could only be easier for the staff if they were to meet in regular curricular discussions, although it is surprising to find frequently that this does not occur. If the headteacher does not take the lead and organize such meetings, then although the infant and junior staffs might socialize informally they are unlikely to go into depth to co-ordinate curriculum planning and review. Often the role may be delegated to a holder of a 'post of special responsibility', but the headteacher will still need to keep a finger on the pulse by ensuring regular feedback.

Unfortunately, children can pass from one class to another, as well as from the infant to junior department, with very little continuity in some subject areas (Bennett *et al*, 1984). Improvement appears to be occurring in some schools as a result of the current moves requiring schools to evaluate performance more closely and state their goals. Where infant and junior schools are separate, then far more effort is needed on the part of headteachers, in particular, to co-ordinate and plan for continuity. There is a need for the staff in both schools to be aware of and committed to an overall and agreed plan for continuity and long-term policies. Resources, such as published schemes etc, can often be built up and shared, easing the expense and fostering continuous education for each child.

Where the schools are separate or the departments are located on separate sites, staff from the infant schools will find it difficult to get to know the staff from the junior schools they feed, and conversely the same applies. In large schools this can happen even when situated on the same campus. Reading and mathematics schemes are sometimes completely different due to individual autonomies being allowed to prevail. In many cases, the staff's expectations of the children they teach are misplaced. This can be corrected by a better understanding of what each is aiming to do and where the meeting points must be, and this can only be achieved by a total commitment from headteachers and all their staff to understanding the need for continuity in the educational processes. Hadow, as long ago as 1931, noted that 'teachers in lower junior classes should have some knowledge of infant methods'.

Initial teacher training now offers courses covering the three-to-nine age range, which does give junior teachers some insight into infant approaches and vice versa. Many teachers did not get this opportunity and it is now the policy in some schools to give staff the opportunity to change age ranges; this is usually only feasible when the age ranges come under the management of one headteacher, as in a JMI school. For all, however, especially where the staff are in separate campuses, school-based in-service training and inter-school visiting by staff needs to be given a higher priority. Team building courses, which involve the school governors, could form the framework of joint staff meetings for teachers whether from one building or a number of sites. It is especially important that 'post-holders', and others who may have specific responsibilities for continuity, arrange regular meetings between staff of the schools involved to review and discuss the work and needs of those establishments. This would inevitably encroach on the time teachers need to spend outside their classrooms, therefore if difficulties in setting up sufficient full meetings are encountered, at least the post-holders could meet regularly and act as information filters to all concerned.

Ways must be found to minimize the unacceptable practices of children being forced to repeat topics covered in the infant departments. This is not to say that a certain amount of repetition may not be necessary to aid reinforcement, provided that this is properly planned. Perhaps the argument currently prevailing concerning a universal common curriculum may avert some of the problems, but the problem often arises in relation to the methods and materials used for teaching rather than the curriculum aims and framework.

Bennett *et al* (1984) found that there was a high degree of inappropriate matching between the tasks and the children to whom they were given. In this detailed research of the demands made by teachers in both junior and JMI schools, it would appear that the matching of the task to the child was better in the JMI situation. Both high and low achievers suffered from this mismatching, but the overestimation of low achievers was more marked in junior schools than in junior departments of JMI schools. No reason was put forward for this, but it seems very likely that it was because the staff in the JMI school had far better knowledge of what the child had already covered in the earlier classes within their school.

RECORDS

Record keeping is essential if education is to be a continuous process. It is of equal importance within a school as between schools to ensure that details of a child are available to accompany its progress through the various transfers which take place. Time needs to be devoted both by infant and junior staff to agreeing, preferably by consensus, what the content ought to be and the format it should take. Records should be available for use for all the more obvious reasons but also to make optimum use of the experiences of previous staff who have put time and effort into keeping information which will aid continuity in the child's progress. A teacher receiving a child on the next step of the educational ladder needs to know what that child has or has not done or achieved and what has been tried and experienced. In addition, the teacher needs to have an indication of any problems or difficulties the child might have had. A checklist is often devised by staff, but whatever the format, teaching information needs to be factual, easily accessible, current and usable rather than based on a subjective and, sometimes, unsubstantiated opinion of a child's potential. Some form of 'profiling' would be worth considering by staff when reviewing their record keeping systems; this would be particularly appropriate in the present climate where many secondary schools are beginning to use profiling for recording both subject and 'social' progress. Teachers who have worked through their own needs and who have been involved in developing their own recording systems, undoubtedly have a far higher commitment to making their system work.

Nothing need be recorded on a child's record that the parents cannot share and, *provided that they are involved and kept fully informed*, there should be no reason for them to be surprised by anything contained in such records. If a child is experiencing difficulties then the sooner parents are aware of this the better: it may well be that the need to record information could provide a teacher with the opportunity to bring this tactfully to the parents' notice.

Conclusions concerning the first compulsory schooling stage

From the information given both in this chapter and Chapter 1, there is a strong case for joint planning of the curriculum and recording systems for children from the age of three right through to 11 years of age by all concerned – ideally this could well be extended to 16 years, as will be seen in the next part of this book. Indeed, in response to the DES circular *The School Curriculum* (June 1981), many Local Education Authorities have set up working parties to formulate curriculum guidelines for the entire age range. Other LEAs have been more prescriptive and a few have disregarded this altogether! If, and when, these schemes are implemented then, at long last, planned continuity will surely become much more the norm for every child.

To conclude this examination of the second bridge, continuity will improve when all those involved are not only aware of its importance, but are fully committed to creating and maintaining the systems necessary. Recently, there have been signs of much improvement as is illustrated by the examples described in Chapter 6. Equally, parents are a key factor in these transitions and they need to be both fully involved in the processes necessary and helped to understand their vital role. Only when common

ground is fully established will a child's education be truly continuous.
As Dean (1985) says,

> We have given lip-service to the idea of continuity. Cintinuity will only happen when our commitment is sufficient to give it a high level of priority. There is a VERY REAL NEED TO DO SO!

CHAPTER 3
FROM PRIMARY TO SECONDARY SCHOOLING

Moving to the big school

In this chapter, we have reached what is for most children in many educational systems, the biggest step in moving from one phase to another of the process – the transition from junior to secondary or middle to secondary schooling. Because of the complexity of our system and the variations in LEA policies, the age at which a child may take this major step will vary considerably. Some authorities have a three-tier system involving transfer to middle schools as an intermediary step, but the majority still maintain a two-tier system. For many children the introduction of middle schools alleviated much of the trauma experienced by some of the 'great divide', as the separation between the primary and secondary sectors has often been called. If there is to be continuity, how best can this 'great divide' be bridged and what problems are we likely to have to overcome? These are some of the issues which are explored in this part of the examination of transition and continuity in the educational process.

The different routes which children may take and the number of times they may change schools require 'more effort to establish and maintain continuity and coherence in what children learn and are expected to achieve' (HMI report 1980, *A View of the Curriculum*). In a similar way, this was also observed by Youngman (1980), who wrote,

> All education experience involves pupils in some kind of adjustment to new situations or demands but the strength and variety of influences encountered during transfer make this a particularly important stage in education.

The fact that Plowden (1967) devoted a complete chapter to continuity and consistency between stages of education, gives credit to the notion that it demands considerable attention. There were several recommendations on how to bridge the gap, such as: 'there should be contact between teachers in primary and secondary schools', 'parents should be known in their secondary schools' and 'records need to be passed on', all of which will be examined later in this chapter. Having established the importance of this step and the fact that it is worthy of far more consideration than it is apparently getting, what, then, are some of the problems and in what areas might some improvements be made?

For education to be seen as a continuum, each stage must be seen as a component of the total process. It is important to consider carefully the child's experiences in the previous stages and those likely to be had in the stage that follows. This has been advocated by many educational theorists such as Dewey (1938) and, more recently, Bruner (1960) in his 'spiral curriculum', who stated 'that one experience should follow another in a sequence of meaningful learning'. Likewise, the theme continues today as is found in a recent DES report in the statement,

> ... to deal adequately with pupils within one phase of education requires a thorough understanding of the educational needs of children in that age range and a view of how a particular phase relates to the whole process. (*The Curriculum 5-16*, DES, 1985)

This document could be extended to embrace the 3-16 age range, since more emphasis is now given to the earlier years than was formerly the case, although there is still a long way to go. If it is agreed that continuity of experience is of the utmost importance then a more detailed look must be taken at what actually happens in practice and what needs to be done to smooth out the passage for all pupils.

Children's attitudes

'You've been a big fish in a small pool, now you'll be a small fish in a big lake' – a familiar saying and one which could easily unnerve a child looking ahead to the secondary school. The negative aspects of transfer are all too obvious; the change from a small to a large school, from having one teacher based in one familiar classroom, to having to cope with many new faces in different rooms, with both different teachers and fellow schoolchildren.

However, in reality, many children enjoy this change: new subjects, new friends, a sense of moving 'up' and a feeling of reaching an important step in their lives.

Consider some actual comments made by children before and after this transfer:

before:
> 'It's going to be very big and there's all those new teachers and different lessons . . . you might get lost!'
> 'You have lots of homework!'
> 'I might not be with my friends.'
> 'They don't let you out of the classrooms to go to the toilet!'
> 'And your head's flushed down the toilet!!!'

after:
> 'I was really scared on the first day – I didn't sleep properly.'
> 'There were so many people, but you soon get used to it.'
> 'I didn't think that I would understand the timetable but we sorted it out.'
> 'It's funny how you think it's big, but it's ever so easy really.'

There is, then, a need to prepare children for the moment of transition and to ensure that they settle into their new environment once they have made the transfer. Some children find the transfer to secondary school very easy; they are ready for the change and may even perceive it as a challenge. There are a few children, on the other hand, who are so over-anxious that they experience all kinds of worries before they leave the junior phase and have a traumatic time when they arrive at the new school. These children need personal and expert help if they are to settle and benefit from the wide range of educational and recreational activities on offer.

There are very few children who have no qualms at all about changing schools and those who seem completely confident are often hiding their feelings of apprehension. It is possible to group the main anxieties into a number of main issues. Measor and Woods in their book *Changing Schools* (1984) found that pupil's anxieties revolved around five main issues:

— the size and more complex organization of the new school,
— new forms of discipline and authority,
— new demands of work,
— the prospect of being bullied,

— the possibility of losing one's friends.

The responsibility for easing children's anxieties is shared by the junior, middle and secondary schools and the effort and care that go into meeting this responsibility can be seen in the various programmes which are increasingly being developed by schools in many LEAs. In 1977, Jennings and Hargreaves carried out some research in Sheffield into children's attitudes to secondary school transfer. At that time the LEAs were introducing middle schools into some areas. The study was carried out using a standardized questionnaire before and after transfer, as well as an open-ended 'essay' analysis. Their results clearly showed that transition from junior to secondary schooling had detrimental short-term effects upon the attitudes of children, compared with those who moved to middle schools as an intermediary step. Further research would be needed to determine whether these short-term effects have any long-term consequences – the educational consequences could be far reaching. It is also worth speculating that, since this LEA was in the process of introducing middle schools, it was likely that more care than usual was probably being taken over these transition stages. It is therefore possible that the consequences of transition nationwide are significantly worse than was found in this research.

Historical background

In looking back to the 1930s, we can consider how far we have really progressed in strengthening the primary and secondary educational links. The Hadow Report had a liberating effect on the primary school curriculum, recommending far more activity and experience-based learning. This was followed by *The Spens Report on Secondary Education* (1938), suggesting that:

> . . . in the secondary school the pupil's studies must be retrospective in so far as they are based on what has gone before,

as well as stating,

> . . . prospective in so far as they look forward to maturer studies.

What better model for defining continuity at the primary to secondary transition interface could there be? Unfortunately, World War II took the nation's concentration and energies away from education and schooling, to a major extent, to problems associated with evacuation, etc.

The 1944 Education Act changed the Hadow recommendation of an elementary and higher approach to education, to a 'tri-partite' system based on primary, secondary and further sectors with selection at the age of 11 years. This Act stressed that education should be a continuous process but this mandatory break at 11 into different forms of secondary education, namely 'grammar', 'technical' and 'secondary modern', provided for *anything but continuity*. Many children experienced dramatic changes, particularly those selected for the grammar schools. Pressures on primary schools to prepare their pupils for the 11+ examination frequently led to the exclusion of much of the activity- and experience-based approaches from the curriculum, in favour of more formal examination-orientated instruction in order to secure grammar school successes. Pupils experienced discontinuity in curriculum programmes when entering this secondary sector and being introduced to subjects such as Latin, physics, etc; craft-based curriculae were predominantly the province of the technical and secondary modern schools.

It is true that in the vast majority of authorities selection by 11+ no longer exists, however, even with the advent of 'comprehensive' education, do the expectations of some secondary teachers lead them to disregard totally what has gone before and start anew by using some means of assessing attainment in order to 'classify' or 'stream' their charges? With so many classes to be organized for each year, it is inevitable that some form of 'selection' is likely to be used, at or shortly after reception, to group children into more or less homogeneous groupings; initially, tests of past achievement rather than potential are one option! In the 1960s there was increasing awareness of the problems of continuity and the suggestion made in the Plowden Report for the introduction of 'middle' schools was seen as an effective bridge between the primary and secondary stages of education:

> It [Middle school education] must move forward into what is now regarded as Secondary school work, but it must not move so far away that it loses the best of Primary education as we know it now . . . (paragraph 383)

Five years prior to Plowden, Sir Alec Clegg, then the Chief Education Officer for the West Riding of Yorkshire, introduced the middle school system to relieve problems of overcrowding in urban areas. His committee's motives were not entirely concerned with continuity, but headteachers from all sectors were involved in the decision-making process and agreed that children between the ages of 9 and 11 years would benefit from a more gradual introduction to secondary schooling. Age of transfer now varies according to where the children happen to live and depends on the LEA policies. Even within LEAs it is usual for a mixture of systems to exist. For example, in one forward thinking authority every combination can be seen. In this authority it is possible for children to move schools at 7, 8, 9, 11, 12 and 13 years of age because there are junior schools for ages 7-11 and middle schools for both ages 8-12 and 9-13. We can only feel sympathy for the children and parents who live on the boundaries of catchment areas, or who have to move schools for relocation reasons. The big advantage of middle schools, as one would expect, is that pupils do not seem to suffer such marked discontinuities from transfer, as is borne out by the Jennings and Hargreaves study (1977). Some children may find transfer at eight or nine years of age somewhat daunting, although the teaching philosophies and methods in the early years of middle schools are often closer to those of primary than secondary schools. The study of Stillman and Maychell (1984) carried out in Isle of Wight middle schools and other schools found that liaison and adaptation by pupils was easier, but that curriculum continuity still presented many problems. It is clear that this 'hotch-potch' provision needs more attention both at national and local levels to promote more continuity in the educational process if the child's needs are to be met.

Dean (1985) points out that 'schools need some honest assurance, in a time of decreasing numbers on registers, that resources will be available so that they can plan ahead'. This is not easy while education is a 'political football' and party policies are often in conflict. With parents having a wider choice of schools for their children, problems of continuity are likely to increase unless some action is also taken to unify patterns and philosophies.

Finally, it cannot be ignored that purely educational objectives can conflict with the economic viability of schools. Often compromises must be made to ensure that schools can be operated with acceptable numbers of pupils to teaching staff while at the same time optimizing the costs of the resources deployed. In some areas demographic changes are taking place so rapidly that closures of schools and the establishment of temporary accommodation will perpetually cause continuity problems.

Liaison and curriculum continuity

Transition from primary to secondary school can be viewed from two different aspects – liaison and continuity. Liaison can be far easier to achieve as it does not directly have to involve the curriculum. Indeed, the majority of secondary schools have some form of liaison with their feeder schools, at least immediately prior to entry if not earlier.

While the subsequent parts of this chapter concentrate on the transition from primary to secondary school, this being by far the most common option for pupils, most of what is stated applies to transitions involving middle schools. It is true, however, for reasons stated in the previous section that the middle school transfers do seem to be better handled on the whole.

LIAISON

This can take various forms and some of the main (good) practices are highlighted below:

a) Pupils are invited to spend some time in the secondary school during the summer term prior to their transfer. This can include various activities, but the main purpose is to familiarize pupils with the building, some organizational characteristics and to meet some of the older pupils and, particularly, some key staff.
b) The head of the first year will often visit the primary schools to meet pupils and to discuss any fears and anxieties they might have and reassure them on various routines.
c) First-year pupils return to their primary schools to talk with those about to transfer.
d) Parents of new entrants are invited to the secondary school for a formal introductory meeting and, perhaps, for social functions during the year.
e) Information in the form of letters and school brochures is circulated in good time so that parents can ask questions on areas of concern.
f) Open days for the new starters and their parents are specially arranged in conjunction with the feeder schools.

CURRICULUM CONTINUITY

This aspect is much more difficult to achieve but attempts are being made by many schools. The success depends entirely upon the commitment of the headteachers and the staff of all schools involved, both primary and secondary. If we now look at some of the discontinuities, it is easy to see why this is such a difficult task even when the will to do something constructive exists.

If it is accepted that 'a concept of education as a continuous process, irrespective of major changes of school' (Plowden, 1967) is the ideal for each child, how realistically can it be achieved in practice? More effort needs to be made to investigate and resolve the possible problems, for, as Marland (1977) found, much of the lip-service paid to continuity 'is time consuming and is unproductive activity'.

The main reasons for the existence of these discontinuities appear to be:

a) Many primary and secondary teachers perceive a difference in their philosophies, such as, for example, child-centred versus subject-centred approaches.

b) Little notice is frequently taken of information passed on in the form of records and all too often little regard is paid to past experiences. This results in pupils starting all over again at the same or a lower level, or, possibly worse, false assumptions being made about attained knowledge. In *The Curriculum 5–16* (1985), it was found that this was most apparent between the transition from primary to secondary schools, as is stated in the document – '. . . it brings with it the risks of unprofitable repetition and narrow teaching, because of the lack of a well-informed appreciation of what has gone before. The tendency is to assume that children have learnt little. If, as a result, the teaching reverts to an undemanding level for the pupils, then disillusionment and boredom can set in'. How crucial this is for all children, but in particular for children with special needs.

c) There are still too many teachers who overprotect their personal autonomy in their classroom and this seems to apply particularly to some schools which also tend to insularity as a whole. The Isle of Wight research by Stillman found that only 13 per cent of 1,507 teachers actually participated in curricular discussions with their receiving schools, although 94 per cent believed that their work should be properly linked.

d) Organizational constraints are numerous. For example, one of the most difficult to overcome is where many primary schools feed several secondary schools all of whose catchments overlap. These make curriculum continuity almost impossible, unless all can be involved, because of the lack of integrated policy-making between schools. This is even further compounded where the schools are in different authorities. The current moves towards a National Curriculum must surely help to alleviate some of these problems.

e) All too often, primary teaching is still considered by some within and many outside the profession as inferior to secondary teaching. The lower the age range of the teaching, the stronger this perception appears to apply.

f) Parents are not given recognition by professionals for the part they can play in supporting continuity.

These observations are reinforced by the research of Stillman and Maychell (1984). They refer to four main problem areas: attitudes across sectors, liaison meeting skills, curriculum issues and assessment for transfer.

The major issue of concern during the transfer from primary to secondary schooling, surely, must be that of the continuity of the curriculum. However, we see more attention paid to liaison for a 'smooth passage' and because curriculum continuity is so much more difficult to implement, it is given a 'back seat' or despaired over.

Liaison is much easier to put into practice and, undoubtedly, is essential as a forerunner to curriculum continuity. Is this latter issue so difficult for teachers to perceive? Probably so, if both primary and secondary teachers view it from their own perspectives. Lois Benyon (1984), after considerable research, suggests 'there was an immense need to get more accurate knowledge about what the other side did and why'.

In Chapter 2, it was highlighted that there was often a lack of continuity between classes in the same school and now it is even more apparent that this exists to a far greater extent between schools. The HMI report *A View of the Curriculum* (1980) states that 'more effort is needed to establish and maintain continuity and coherence in what children learn and are expected to achieve'.

Since the great majority of LEAs abolished selection at 11+, many primary schools often went diverse ways in their choice of curriculum, although there was usually some commonality in the core subject areas. With some secondary schools receiving children from upwards of 20 primary schools and, conversely, some primary schools feeding nine or more secondary schools, the problem of curriculum continuity is virtually impossible to resolve at school level. The 1988 Education Act giving parents more choice over the selection of schooling for their children, can only compound the problems, however, we must continually look for ways to improve this in practice. This will involve, perhaps, the use of third parties who would stand a better chance of viewing the whole process impartially, such as the LEA, HMI or DES. This was touched on in the DES document *A View of the Curriculum* (1980). Certainly, where schools are suitably geographically situated then great strides can be made towards continuity (see Chapter 6). The primary school philosophy of child-centredness must provide secondary school teachers with a tremendous task when trying to structure their intake.

While the cliché 'primary schools teach children whereas secondary schools teach subjects' is patently incorrect, it does illustrate why curriculum continuity is difficult to achieve. When considering the individual autonomy of teachers and the different approaches between schools, any curriculum continuity which does take place represents a major achievement. It is little wonder that there is constant criticism from all sides of children 'marking time', 'repeating work', 'given work that is too easy/difficult' and 'jumping or missing out steps in learning'. These criticisms do not just relate to knowledge acquisition but also to development of skills and attitudes. In *A View of the Curriculum* (1980) one of the aims expressed is, 'to ensure that comparable expectations are being established about the range of experience and performance of pupils at a given stage', so, if the concern is with 'experience and performance', then the teacher is involved in the whole area of concepts, skills and values. Indeed, the emphasis should constantly be on the stage which the pupil has reached building on the individualization of learning.

Where there is good practice in curriculum continuity, it is usually in the subject areas of mathematics and language – this is because of the emphasis of sequential learning in the former and the structured approach to the teaching of language, and in particular reading, in recent years. For these reasons, the stress on planning for continuity across the two stages of education in these curriculum areas is much easier and sequential progression can often be achieved.

Stillman and Maychell (1984) chose language as one area where it would be easier to see a linear structure across the 5-16 age range. They suggest that:

... if curriculum and continuity respects each child's progression through a series of learning avenues within each subject then we can see that structure and overall planning are necessary if a coherent end product is to be reached.

Improvements

Having established that there is a lack of curriculum continuity across the primary to secondary bridge of transition, what then can be done to improve the situation? There are pockets of good practice, which will be described later, but it is important first to turn to more general observations on how improvement could begin. The word 'begin' is important because any change is going to be a slow process given the nature of this problem. Having recognized this, in the simple act of seeking to overcome the difficulties the essential start has already been made. Recognition and commitment must precede action. The first major step is in the establishment of suitable mechanisms to start the process of liaison between a secondary school and its feeder schools. Once this is done, the climate is right to explore possible guidelines for curriculum continuity. In doing this the role of the headteacher is crucial and all involved must fully understand what is required and be totally committed and willing to be closely involved.

Having said this, the following are the main events which need to take place.

a) Each school will need to review its aims and objectives in the different curriculum areas. In fact, many schools have already embarked on this with the assistance of the LEAs in order to produce continuity in the curriculum for the years 3-16, in response to the DES circular 6/81.
b) It is advisable to look at one area at a time due to the amount of time and organization required.
c) Joint meetings between primary and secondary members of staff will need to be set up and led by post holders and heads of department or subjects.
d) Preparation will be needed to help teachers – probably by means of in-service training – in negotiating, mediating, guiding skills and in conducting meetings, if they are to keep on target and the outcomes are to be effectively thought through. Finding mutually acceptable time will be difficult, but it often provides an excellent opportunity to visit each other's schools.

e) In order to promote good continuity in any area, record keeping is essential. For this to be effective, records must be kept in such a way that they give the required information quickly, accurately and in a usable format. They will need to be carefully designed and mutually agreed.

Records

The whole subject of record keeping will be dealt with in more detail in Chapter 7, but some discussion is included here because of its importance in this context.

To counteract the fact that children's progress should not be slow, or even regress after transfer, 'the passage of information is an essential part of the transfer system' (The Thomas Report, *Improving Primary Schools*, 1985). However, this report does go on to say that written information in itself is never enough, implying that much more communication between teachers and parents is necessary. Indeed, inter-school visiting between teachers can help considerably to ensure that written records are properly understood through discussion, which is vitally important when grades and results need some explanation, as is so often the case. This applies particularly to information concerning children with 'Special Needs' as mere written information rarely copes with all the nuances necessary to explain the needs which they are likely to have or accurately describe past progress. The Fish Report (ILEA, 1985) states that:

> Provision should be made for regular and reciprocal visits by teachers in neighbouring Primary and Secondary Schools so that they may become familiar with the curriculum and organisation of each other's schools.

It must be stressed that children from ethnic minorities often require much more attention when their records are compiled or interpreted. What often seems a problem for these children, frequently results from a lack of real understanding of their language and cultural norms.

As indicated earlier, records will only be effective if they are used and properly understood by the child's new teacher. If they are accessible and the information is quickly extracted, then not only does the child benefit but all the hard work put into the production of these records by the former teacher is then worth while. One sheet of simple format providing all the essential information and possibly a 'profile' of the child is more likely to get attention than a wordy document. The assessment guidelines given by Stillman and Maychell (1984) serve as a well-proven basis (see Chapter 7). In liaison, teachers need to devote much thought to devising a suitable, yet simple, standard method of recording what work has been covered in the primary school as well as trying to ensure that there is continuity in the curriculum. More difficult is the recording of those inbuilt personal qualities that are so essential to success: the child's reactions to challenges and opportunities in education and where to support weaknesses by seeking out the causes.

To stress again, written records will nearly always need to be supported by discussion, even though this takes time.

Conclusions concerning this transition

Having looked at the difficulties and problems which children may experience when crossing this 'Great Divide', where can improvements be made in practice? Liaison at its best must be about human relationships and a thorough understanding between teachers, pupils and parents. Findlay stated in 1985:

> It seems an easier concept to handle than continuity since it relates to events which happen in real-time and an identifiable number of procedures exist which are designed to get children from one sector of education to another.

Indeed, this is borne out by many practices and preparations for transfer in many areas of the country. Continuity is much harder to achieve, as has been stated, and until primary and secondary philosophies can be brought more closely together, it is difficult to see how it can happen. I believe that this cannot be confined to the curriculum alone, but must include children's and parents' attitudes, organization, teacher's skills and teaching philosophies and methods – achievable if each is tackled one at a time depending on which is seen as the particular priority locally and in agrement with the other schools in the transitional process. (Examples of co-operative approaches are described in Chapter 6)

In the keeping of records, all these areas need careful consideration as they should accompany children into (and possibly throughout, in certain circumstances) their secondary phase of education. Records, then, can be used to establish the link between liaison and continuity. As Findlay (1985) points out, 'good liaison practices are the tip of the curriculum continuity iceberg'.

The constraints placed on secondary schools with regard to examination pressures is appreciated, but does it really need to begin in the first year? What, if any, influence should examinations and tests have on the curriculum in the junior or early secondary years? It would seem that it could be possible to continue the best of primary practices in the first two years of secondary school by effectively treating these years as an 'internal' middle school. While heads of department cling to their territories and refuse to cross boundaries this will not happen. This is well highlighted in the following extract from *The Practical Curriculum* (DES, 1981, p 52),

> ... the problem of ensuring continuity and progression transcends subject boundaries, just as it transcends the boundaries between stages of schooling. Finding ways of monitoring continuity and progression would be one of the best ways of providing the child with an effective curriculum!

A curriculum designed for the upper junior and lower secondary phase must include competence, confidence and co-operation. Should 'learning to learn' be the corner-stone of school work, considering how fast human knowledge and technology are moving? To achieve a broadly conceived policy for this phase, teachers need to take advantage of the ever widening opportunities to develop genuine curriculum continuity which, initially, entails having real respect for each other's skills, knowledge and practices. LEAs and headteachers should be aware of this need and allow for the release of primary and secondary teachers with curriculum responsibility to meet each other in school time. This should happen both in their respective schools and through activities under the umbrella of in-service training provision. Some catalyst needs to prompt the majority of schools to get started by giving help, guidance and training in what is required. From my own observations, teacher exchange between primary and secondary schools has been very effective in obtaining a better understanding of the part each sector plays in the educational process and the problems caused by discontinuity. This exchange is not difficult to arrange given the appropriate commitment of the teachers involved. As Dean (1985) says, 'the sacrifice of professional autonomy seems inevitable if curriculum continuity is to be attempted'.

I frequently state that it is my firm belief that the role of parents is very much under-valued where transition and continuity in their children's education are concerned. Parents need to be brought together with primary and secondary teachers through induction programmes; this would certainly allay some of their fears about their children's change of schools, for example, and provide them with a much better understanding of the real issues on which their selection of school should be made.

The more information which can be shared, the better the understanding is likely to be of what the schools are trying to achieve. There is a real need for a 'contract' type of approach between schools and parents concerning their children's education – each being fully informed on progress and planning throughout. It is important that each recognizes the extent of their specific accountabilities, particularly those relating to behaviour, attitudes and motivation.

Finally, the early secondary years should provide an excellent opportunity for teachers to adapt and capitalize on the children's feelings of excitement, challenge and change. With a breadth of curriculum and a teacher of general subjects, together with some introduction of specialisms, a child could have the best of both worlds and the period of adjustment would be an enjoyable one. Seeing education as a continuum implies that there are gradual, almost imperceptible changes which take the infant through to adolescence and far beyond, if their learning experiences have been enjoyable and satisfying.

CHAPTER 4
THROUGH SECONDARY TO 16 AND BEYOND

The variety of provision

The main form of provision at the secondary stage is by various sorts of comprehensive systems, the main exceptions being where a few LEAs have retained selection systems at 11+ for entry into selective 'grammar' schools. Even these exceptions are not consistent across any of the retaining LEAs since the option is often restricted to local rather than authority-wide provision. The grammar school issue only clouds the already complex transitional and curriculum problem in these localities even more. Added pressures exist for both pupils and parents, not only in the selection process but also from the social base of the catchment areas in which they might live. The demand for such places far exceeds the number of places available and 'the comprehensive' could be regarded as the place where 'the failures go'. Such confusion of provision gets even worse when considering that, in addition to the conventional state-controlled sector, there are 'Church' schools and the increasingly available direct grant provision of the private and boarding sectors.

Transfer between schools within the secondary system, therefore, is full of pitfalls, not just because of the differences in curriculum and emphasis which can be expected between the secondary schools, but also because of the radical differences of philosophy which can exist. Clearly, for the highly mobile family there is a very real problem once children reach the secondary stage as to what to do.

It is salutory to recognize that a primary school may well have to prepare children for all the possible school curricula and cultures which could all exist within its transfer area.

Finally, in the introduction to this chapter it must also be stated that there is a whole sector of the school population that will require special provision. There are those children who have special needs and whose degree of need may make it impossible for them to integrate either directly or by means of 'special units' into the conventional secondary sector. This highly specialist area is not part of the content of this book and is only mentioned because it does highlight yet another transitional problem that can occur when a handicap is provided for by integration in one area but not in another. The distress which can result can be very unsettling for all concerned.

Constraints of subject orientation

It has long been accepted that one of the principle discontinuities between primary and secondary schools is the constraint imposed by the subject orientation of the secondary curriculum. The organizational structures of most secondary schools are based on the departments controlling groups of subject areas, for example languages, science, and mathematics, etc. There is no standard way in which these subject groupings take place, much seems to depend on the past traditions of the school and the overall size; this is a far cry from the child-centred approach of nearly all primary schools where the emphasis is on a cross-curricular teaching approach to the required areas in the curriculum.

To a large extent the subject-orientated approach has evolved in the secondary sector as a result of the need to meet the rigid requirements imposed by the various subject examinations and the criteria of the examination bodies themselves. The current review of the examination system and vocational qualifications is the first major attempt to bring some rationalization to this situation. Unfortunately it is likely to be a long process, if only because of the time scales between a pupil starting a course and completing the process. Transitions of methodology even within a subject can be very complex, as is vividly demonstrated by the introduction of the GCSE. Organizationally, it is unlikely that it will be possible to change from a subject-grouped departmental structure and it is doubtful whether this would even be desirable in view of the stronger subject emphasis of the post-16 sector.

A final constraining factor is the need for access to very specialist subject facilities in the secondary curriculum, such as laboratories; these will always need close control by appropriately qualified teaching and non-teaching support staff.

This subject orientation seems to have been eased to some extent where 'middle' schools have been established. Often it is the aim of such organizations in the first two years to provide security in the shape of a class teacher who is responsible for the welfare of the children and the majority of their lessons will be given in their self-contained 'year areas' (home base!). They are gradually prepared for the third and fourth years, which are designed to be more subject-based, by having increasing contact with specialist teachers in working areas who have the necessary facilities. This undoubtedly eases the transition from strong involvement with one generalist teacher to the need to become associated with many specialist teachers. Such preparation has started in some junior schools where they are large enough to justify introducing pupils to specialist teachers. More often these are in the areas of music, practical subjects and physical activities requiring the use of specialized facilities.

It must be noted that where there is severe economic contraction associated with falling rolls, inconsistencies between intentions and practices with regard to establishing continuity frequently occur. Invariably such demographic changes can be predicted and must be planned for well in advance, principally by the LEAs, if good practice can be established.

Concern over this transition from being taught by the 'generalist' to the 'specialist' was highlighted in the DES, HMI *Primary Report* in 1978, and more recently in the University Council for the Education of Teachers Report of 1982.

Perceived roles of secondary teachers

There has been much consideration given recently to the discontinuities which occur as a result of the different perceptions that exist between primary and secondary teachers. Much of this comes into sharp focus when primary curriculum co-ordinators meet heads and teachers in the corresponding subject disciplines to discuss and learn about each other's work. This often occurs as a result of in-service training sessions or planning 'workshops'.

Where secondary teachers are highly qualified specialists, it can be a daunting prospect to be asked to teach across a wider range of curriculum areas rather than remain within the parameters of their own disciplines. Inevitably, this is likely to be more and more demanded of them with the potential restriction of specialist options which could prevail as a result of the government emphasis on a broader based education with, however, a stronger emphasis on a narrower range of 'core subjects'.

Frequently teachers' style, method of tuition and content structure are determined by the examination end points for which they are preparing their pupils. As will be discussed in Chapter 7, this situation is rapidly changing with the advent of such approaches as the Certificate of Pre-Vocational Education (CPVE), the Technical and Vocational Education Initiative (TVEI), and other cross-curricular schemes.

Primary teachers have often been described as 'jacks of all trades and masters of none' – their spread of subjects makes it very demanding for them to specialize in a subject in depth; this frequently results in a communication difficulty between the primary and secondary teacher when discussing the transition and curriculum requirements which can provide the pupil with the chance of a smooth passage through the secondary school system. The biggest step forward is where the secondary school is designing its first-year programmes of teaching in collaboration with the teachers from its feeder schools. This is now occurring in a number of pilot areas and must augur well for the future of phased curriculum continuity as a structured and planned approach (see Chapter 6).

Progression through the secondary system

Much of a child's progress through the secondary system depends on such a wide variety of factors that it is difficult to determine which have the greatest effect.

The primary and probably most significant factors, since all others seem to hinge around them, are concerned with simple genetics and who the pupil's parents happen to be. A lot depends on the attitudes and support of parents, or the parental figures in their absence, and the nurture they provide to the child's development. Given that the appropriate opportunities and experiences are provided at the right time by all those who are involved in the child's development process, progress through the system should be relatively smooth; in such a climate a child should be able to realize his or her optimum capability. Sadly, this is not always the case; the adults who are in control are not always sufficiently perceptive or capable of establishing the right environment. With some parents there may be a 'blindness' which impedes their judgement when it comes to assessing what is best for their own children.

Even when all the human factors are of the highest standard, regrettably the material ones may be beyond the adult's means. However, although money is often seen as the answer to many problems, there are as many examples of its misuse as of its benefits in setting up helpful opportunities for children.

As teachers, we are obligated to make good use of the skills and opportunities we can give to our pupils. By being aware of the many discontinuities in intellectual, physical, social and emotional development during childhood and adolescence, we can minimize the disruption which occurs throughout the educational system, and provide positive and beneficial influences. Fortunately, the profession seems to be moving towards a far greater awareness of pupils' needs and is making good progress towards meeting them.

Measures to prevent overspecialization at an early age and to begin to rationalize some of the 16+ qualifications, while widening their scope, seem to be progressing in the right direction. However, decisions taken at an early age have sometimes caused pupils to be carried along inappropriate curricular paths which subsequently lead to later career or academic problems. Clearly, the chances of a child being able to perceive a long-term career path during his or her time at school are diminishing with advances in technology. A recent survey indicates that less than 50 per cent of adults aged 25 are in a job which they determined early in their secondary school days, and that more than 75 per cent view their curriculum subjects – apart from core subjects like mathematics, English and appropriate sciences – as not at all relevant to their later careers. There is, of course, a danger of taking a purely materialistic view of the learning process; it is quite often difficult, in later life, to see the real effect that a 'rounded' education has had.

Of course, we cannot prevent some students from making a bad choice of course and possibly failing, and as a result finding it difficult to get a job or to progress further. Regrettably, employment is not likely to be more readily available in the foreseeable future, especially to those who lack qualifications or appropriate social skills and attitudes. It can also be argued that children should be properly fitted in the future not only to take advantage of employment opportunities, but also of their potential leisure time and social activities. This latter point is already becoming obvious to those who teach in areas of economic decline since it is becoming increasingly difficult to predict the stability of either regional or specific employment opportunities. It is very likely, however, that the amount of leisure time people have will continue to grow and that they will have a varying amount of personal disposable income – we should prepare children as well as we can for this.

Current pressures

There are so many pressures on the educational system that it would be impossible to examine them all in detail in this book. Three areas are covered which are major influences and where the pressures for change are particularly influential regarding transition and continuity: national pressures; parental and local pressures; and industrial, commercial and professional pressures.

NATIONAL PRESSURES

Teachers have often been portrayed as being individually or collectively responsible for the poor academic achievement of school leavers, for indiscipline and poor moral development in young people and for the apparent failure of the educational system to provide the appropriate skills for work. At the same time, they are expected to adapt to significantly changing role definitions and responsibilities. The significant changes which are to be instituted according to the recommendations contained in the GERBIL (Great Education Reform Bill) have, in part, arisen as a result of such criticisms.

The 'Great Debate' aired the growing demand for teachers, schools and the educational authorities to become far more accountable to the public. This was formalized in the 1980 Education Act when:

— parental participation in their schools' governing bodies was increased,
— parental involvement was increased in the selection of a particular school for their child, and,
— schools were required to make their examination results available.

Evaluation then became another pressure – this was sometimes instigated by the school itself but was more often carried out externally by the LEA or as a result of an HMI investigation. Indeed, the DES now publish their own reports on individual schools. Based on such evaluative investigations, the DES has produced many reports recently which define those areas in which improvements should be made, such as *The Primary Report* (1978) and *The First School Report* (*Education 5-9*, 1982), together with others such as *The Curriculum 5-16* (1985).

Returning to the GERBIL, the emphasis on the National Curriculum will impose pressures on both schools and teachers which, provided they are well thought through, are new and desirable from the continuity and transition standpoint, and will offer a far greater chance of uniformity between the primary and secondary curriculum contents in individual schools. In addition, the higher level of managerial responsibility and involvement expected of school governors can only benefit the school if they are properly used. Finally, in this Bill the greater the opportunity schools and further education (FE) establishments have to manage their own finances, provided the heads are given adequate training, the more they will be able to allocate resources according to the particular needs of the establishment.

Generally the current 'national' emphasis seems to be both desirable and constructive, although there must be the worry that educational freedom – so long the tradition of UK systems and much admired in other countries – will not be overly restricted. There needs to be sufficient staff and financial resourcing to enable teachers to cope with the changes that are facing them. A good start has been made with the revision of the Local Education Authority Training Grants Scheme (DES Circulars 9 & 10, 1987) for the in-service training of teachers, often referred to as GRIST (Grant Related In-Service Training), which has defined key areas for training and updating purposes, and there are also many additional funding arrangements for specific areas of in-service training activities (eg European Social Fund, MSC/DES grants, DTI funding, CBI initiatives, etc). One major problem is to ensure that there is adequate qualified cover to allow staff to take advantage of such training opportunities. Another problem is how teaching continuity can be maintained in the teacher's class(es) during his or her absence, particularly if it is to be protracted.

Education in the UK is undoubtedly undergoing some of the most major structural and philosophical changes in its history. But with so many changes under way, the worry is that transition and continuity could well feature low on the list of school and LEA priorities, yet implicitly they are *the core of the current national initiatives*.

Parental and local pressures

As has already been mentioned above, the increased power now given to governing bodies and parents in the running of their schools should result in more understanding and greater involvement of parents and the community in the pupil's journey through the educational process. Parents are now questioning the traditional school practices and the educational 'diet' on offer to their children far more. Many have an increased awareness of the opportunities within each syllabus than was at one time the case. In particular, television programmes on educational matters are no longer relegated to off-peak viewing times and are now often designed for the wider population, not only to examine areas of current news interest but also to be entertaining in their own right.

This should encourage all teachers, in particular heads and heads of departments or sections, to update their knowledge and sharpen their thinking and planning so as to ensure that they are moving their pupils towards successful achievement to which the parent can feel commitment.

The benefits of community involvement in pupils' social development is most pronounced where public bodies such as the police, the Health Service, religious institutions and many other organizations can be directly involved in the day-to-day running of the school and are not just seen as organizations that only become involved when 'something goes wrong'. Indeed, these bodies can achieve relations and a degree of understanding which serve as good models and practice for children to follow while contributing to the social educational curriculum of the school.

Industrial, commercial and professional pressures

Some of the main pressures which have caused the current debate and consequent changes that are taking place arise from the public and private business sectors. There is little doubt that many of the traditional curriculums of the recent past were inappropriate to modern commerce. Major changes have taken place, particularly in the post-16 qualifications sector. This started with the formation of the Business Education Council and the Technical Education Council – subsequently combined into the Business and Technical Education Council (BTEC). The organization of this body is heavily weighted so that the content, method and philosophy of the individual curricula are heavily influenced by the appropriate business sector and professional bodies. Other examples include the City and Guilds and the Royal Society of Arts (RSA), which have similar influences. The problem which has all too frequently arisen has been the incompatibility of the qualifications awarded at 16 years of age and the entry requirements needed to go on to post-school studies. Examination bodies have now become involved in a massive re-examination of their syllabi and the interrelationship of courses; the objective is to rationalize what is offered, ensure equality of qualification between bodies and gain acceptance as entry to subsequent educational and training programmes. The main thrust is by means of a National Review of Vocational Qualifications (RVQ) which was set up in 1987 by the National Council for Voactional Qualifications (NCVQ) and is not likely to complete it's work until the mid-1990s.

Employers, often rightly, criticize education for not producing enough people with the qualifications they require. Their involvement in the previously mentioned initiatives can be seen as a major move towards minimizing this problem. The Training Commission seeks to represent their interests, and the degree of financial control they can exert over the funding of education and specific programmes should enable them to do so.

In areas of high technology, for example, it will be difficult for many employers to predict the nature of the qualifications and employment opportunities which will be required in, say, one or two years time – this applies particularly to computing (today transducers, tomorrow . . .). The inevitable outcome of such inability to predict is that the guesses made for curriculum at, say, the age of 12 years, could be drastically incorrect. The implications are that in order to provide for optimum flexibility of later opportunity, many areas of the curriculum will need to be kept open – especially if the pupil is to be able to transfer to courses which will lead to employment opportunities. Unfortunately, the generalization implied in the proposed National Curriculum approach is contrary to the recent early specialism approaches of many secondary schools.

If schools and colleges are to minimize the accusation of producing inappropriately qualified leavers they must ensure that they take full advantage of every opportunity to maintain liaison and dialogue with employers, especially those who are local, both large and small. Such opportunities exist in a variety of forms through parental and social contacts, local business clubs and institute branches – the opportunities are endless. A particular opportunity aimed at bringing employers more closely together within education, mainly, although not exclusively, in the secondary and post-16 sectors, is the recently established Department of Trade and Industry 'Business and Education Initiative' (1987).

Links with post-16 provision

Statutory schooling in the UK finishes at the age of 16, however, for many reasons pupils may remain in the educational system. After discussions with a careers officer, adviser or other persons, the pupil may choose to seek employment in a job sector which is of particular interest. The possibility of employment in that sector depends very much on the availability of work, where the pupil lives or can relocate to and their suitability. Undoubtedly in the South East of England it is generally much easier to find employment, especially for those who are technically competent. Whether a leaver gains employment or not, it is very likely that he or she will still become involved in some form of training or continuing education. Some of this will be qualification-orientated, some purely vocational.

A pupil who is unable to obtain employment at the age of 16 will be offered a place on a suitable Youth Training Scheme (YTS). Since 1986 this opportunity (sponsored by the MSC – now renamed the Training Commission) has become one of the major routes to finding work and work experience and is becoming highly regarded by employers as an appropriate means of converting the leavers to a work ethos. These schemes are run by 'Managing Agents' who negotiate placements with employers, usually local, who are willing to set up and supervise carefully planned training schemes so that trainees can learn the particular business skills required for that type of employment. There are a variety of schemes, but generally all schemes require trainees to undergo a carefully structured training programme which includes theoretical content involving attendance at an approved training college, usually the local college of FE, in conjunction with working for an approved employer. The employer is reimbursed for the costs involved and the trainee receives a weekly allowance for his or her expenses from the MSC; there is no obligation for the employer to subsequently employ the leaver, although this often happens. The theoretical content enables trainees to gain qualifications such as RSA or City and Guilds which enable them to continue to study for additional qualifications.

Instead of seeking work straight after school many students, indeed an increasing number, remain in full-time education either in the sixth-form environment of a secondary school, at (tertiary) sixth-form college or at a college of further education. This transition seems to be relatively smooth providing the earlier subject choices have been well made. Courses at this level usually start afresh which probably alleviates the problem of continuity, and in the past this sector of education has been accustomed to taking a wide variety of entrants and tends to cover a significant amount of ground again early in the new syllabus. This can be very frustrating for some students who feel they are being held back. This problem is beginning to decline with the advent of initiatives such as TVEI and CPVE which, by their very construct, are causing teachers to think far more carefully about the continuity issues.

More students now choose to go to colleges run on further education lines because of their significantly different organization, culture and staff attitudes – these tend to prevail as a result of the teaching traditions of what were originally regarded as technical colleges. The range of courses offered at a FE institution and the prevalence of a considerable number of post-18 part-time and full-time students also widens the 'culture' of FE. The previously mentioned TVEI aims to explore and test ways of organizing and managing the education of 14- to 18-year-olds across the whole ability range so that more of them are attracted to seeking qualifications and skills which will be of direct value to them in preparation for work. This is expected to result in them being better able to acquire practical skills to apply to solving 'real world' problems. This is the only major government-inspired curriculum initiative to receive 100 per cent funding. Most schemes involve schools and are linked with the syllabi and entry requirements of FE or tertiary colleges. Today there are over 50 approved schemes in operation. This represents the first major step forward in establishing proper channels for ensuring continuity from school to further and sixth-form education through to advanced education or employment.

The TVEI approach has led to the setting up of 'pyramids', 'clusters' and 'consortia' (see Chapter 6) involving secondary schools and FE establishments, which are established to ensure continuity of the educational content and processes across the participating establishments – some of these arrangements existed or were in embryonic form before the initiative commenced. The intention is that students should gain a wider range of qualifications than is common in school, particularly in the vocational field. The same staff, especially at managerial levels, are involved in the organizational and curricular process across a wide range of subject areas outside the TVEI sphere. Inevitably, therefore, once the dialogue has been established in the TVEI context it continues quite naturally in the other spheres of activity. Much good work is taking place towards providing adequate guidance for students approaching the age of 16 and sound pastoral support is being established in some areas. All this is encouraging and particularly necessary for those students who, for a variety of reasons, do not receive appropriate support from their home background.

Careers counselling

While careers counselling is very important for students who are unclear about which paths they wish to pursue, it is nevertheless becoming evident that even those who appear decided often make their decisions based on very limited observations. There are two major groups who benefit most – those who have no idea what opportunities there might be for them in the world of work and those who do know but are unsure of how to achieve their goals.

All local authorities have a Careers Service based at central offices but usually with other offices situated in major conurbations. They provide help with information on careers, courses and training opportunities and this is offered by means of confidential counselling interviews with a qualified careers adviser. The staff also have access to lists of job vacancies and training schemes available (such as YTS).

Most secondary schools and colleges will have a suitably trained member of staff who is responsible for careers advice. In the past this person was inadequately trained and lacked the necessary knowledge and experience, but this has changed significantly in recent years, possibly due to initiatives such as CPVE and TVEI. There are now far stronger links with employer organizations and commercial organizations, so outside help can be obtained to supplement the internal advice which is available. Commercial visits, talks and discussions are frequently arranged particularly for the 14- and 15-year-olds.

Most children in the age group 14-16 years have great difficulty in determining what career or study path they might enjoy, simply because they are unaware or unsure of their own skills and latent talents. Equally, their knowledge of the wide range of opportunities for which they might be suited can be very limited. Seldom have they had an opportunity to 'try out' jobs to see how they might feel about them.

There is a wealth of material produced, in written and video form, to assist young people in making their choice, but this can be a bewildering prospect and frequently the services of a Vocational Guidance Assessor will need to be employed. Usually the young person will be subjected to a variety of tests which are designed to provide information on aspects of personal characteristics such as aptitudes, attitudes, areas of interest and so on. Strengths and weaknesses are then established in relation to particular career or training opportunities. The aim is to identify and tailormake the learning programme for individuals so that they meet the necessary requirements to be able to take advantage of those opportunities that are most likely to provide future success and satisfaction. A detailed profile and report is produced and a lengthy debriefing session is offered. Generally, those students who avail themselves of the service find it extremely profitable in their exploration of career opportunities. Some authorities have established such profiling as available to all the pre-GCE (now GCSE) 14- and 15-year-old age group.

CHAPTER 5
PARTICULAR ISSUES

There are a number of specific issues which have been touched on briefly elsewhere in this book and which need further examination – however, they will not be looked at in great detail since each one is a major topic in its own right. The discussion which follows is in the specific context of transition and continuity and has been kept within that context.

Special needs

When seeking to provide equality and opportunity in the educational process for all pupils, we need, perhaps, to define what continuity of provision we make for those who have very special requirements. These pupils may be defined as those who encounter difficulties within the 'normal' school environment unless given special help. Such pupils are not necessarily only those experiencing limitations in their academic achievement but in all aspects of learning; these difficulties can be as a result of prolonged illness, physical and/or mental capacity, social deprivation, antisocial behaviour patterns, domestic or cultural problems and lack of suitable educational opportunities. The children affected range from the especially gifted through to the severely retarded. Often other contributory factors can compound these children's problems, for example having to learn and function in a second language and/or an unfamiliar culture.

The first British legislation to include particular reference to 'Special Education' within the general duties laid down for local authorities was the 1945 Education (Scotland) Act. This stated that these authorities should:

> ... afford all pupils opportunities for education, offering such instruction and training as may be desirable in view of their differing ages, abilities, and aptitudes, and of the differing periods for which they may be expected to remain at school.

Under the earlier 1944 Education Act, children with learning difficulties were assessed by an approved medical officer as suffering from 'a disability of mind or body' – as a result many were placed in 'special schools' and believed to be 'ineducable' regardless of the degree of their handicap. Fortunately we have progressed a long way since then.

In 1970 the Education (Handicapped Children) Act changed this attitude and added the responsibility for the education of the mentally handicapped child to the other educational responsibilities of local authorities, rather than leaving it with the health services. This was further advanced by the DES in a circular it issued in 1975 which recommended new processes of identification and assessment, changing the concept of special education from a medical to an educational context.

It is most likely that the biggest step towards continuity of education for children with special needs came in the report produced by the Warnock Committee in 1978 which provided the impetus for the 1981 Act. This report viewed the scope of special education as a continuum from minor and temporary to major and lasting needs. It sought to establish the concept of 'special provision', where this is made as additional or supplementary to that of general education, rather than as a separate or alternative provision. In the continuity context, it is important to note that this covered children from birth to 19-years-of-age.

A further important factor is that parents are seen as active participants and are counselled and involved throughout the process of establishing the most suitable provision. For some children such provision may be seen to be a 'special school' but these are linked where possible (sometimes as attached 'units') to a mainstream school. A large number of children with special needs are now integrated with their peers in ordinary school classrooms as Warnock recommended.

Assessment techniques have been sharpened as a result of the Warnock report and subsequent legislation in the 1981 Education (Handicapped Children) Act and DES circulars. Recommendations were made concerning the arrangements LEAs needed to make to co-ordinate the work of staff in education with that of other staff from health, social and voluntary services and to ensure that suitable relationships exist. This is an important step forward in terms of continuity in the educational process considering that previously many of these public service departments tended to operate in isolation with very little cross-communication. There is still a great need for further research and development in this field both locally and nationally, particularly to ensure that resources are found to meet those needs, which are now more clearly identifiable, at much earlier ages than hitherto.

A major influence on seeking to provide continuity and progression for pupils with special needs must be the report commissioned and published by the Inner London Education Authority (ILEA). A committee was established, chaired by John Fish (1984), to review special education provision. As a result the report *Educational Opportunities for All* (Fish, 1985) was published. The report is one of three produced by the authority, the others being *Improving Primary Schools* (The Thomas Report, 1985) and *Improving Secondary Schools* (Hargreaves, 1985). This links closely with their aims as referred to elsewhere in this book, but which are worthy of repetition – they are closely allied to those contained in the Warnock Report, namely:

> ... first to enlarge a child's knowledge, experience and imaginative understanding and thus his or her awareness of moral values and capacity for enjoyment; and, secondly, to enable him or her to enter into the world after formal education is over as an active participant in society and as a responsible contributor to it, capable of achieving as much independence as is possible.

This aim is obviously valid for all children but has special implications for those who cannot have the same opportunities for employment and leisure by virtue of their limited learning or physical capacities.

The Fish Report also points out that if many of the intentions of equal (educational) opportunity policies are realized, many more children and young people will have their needs met in schools and colleges. It is important to note that it is not enough that schools and colleges provide equal opportunities, there also needs to be equality of access to such opportunities. Recommendation made by Fish are that clusters, similar to those mentioned in *Improving Primary Schools*, need to be established and that one of the main functions of such a cluster organization should be:

> ... providing a continuity of concern over the child's education, in particular, by facilitating close under-five and primary school links and close secondary and tertiary links in each cluster together with sensitive procedures for transfer from primary to secondary schools.

How does all this 'concern' work in practice? There is an obvious need for more information about the provision and services for the disadvantaged to be made available to parents and various organizations. Children with disabilities or learning difficulties in their early years are being identified much earlier than was thought feasible at one time, and all the various agencies concerned with under-five provision are far more concertedly sharing their expertise than they were in the past. There is still much room, however, for improving the support system for children and parents in many areas. An example of support is where there is a home visiting or teaching counsellor providing systematic early intervention programmes for parents and their children. This has proved invaluable, not just during the early years but in preparing parents and children for the traumatic step into more formal school systems.

Considerable liaison and sharing of information usually precedes entry into nursery or primary school; in particular, placements are carefully considered by educational psychologists, the social services and the appropriate medical advisers. Throughout nursery and primary school and transition into the secondary sector, close contact should be maintained with outside agencies. This is usually a continuing dialogue which should normally involve the parents, the staff of the school and the caring agencies in the progress and needs of the pupil. It was found in the ILEA and elsewhere (Fish, 1985) that there tended to be inadequate support for young people with special needs in the fourth and fifth years of secondary schooling. Many children experienced emotional and behavioural difficulties at this stage and seemed unable to maintain their motivation. Fortunately, the school curriculum is being designed in many schools so that it now provides education in life skills as well as normal curriculum subjects.

Much has been accomplished over recent years to make provision for young people with special needs in colleges and adult education institutions. One example of integration at this level is the involvement of students on 'care' training courses and pupils with special needs – a lot is gained by the exchange of experiences that is of mutual benefit to both parties. The same applies where individuals are placed in 'normal' school classes – here the learning experiences and understanding of the non-special needs pupils are widened by their contact with the special needs children.

Concern still exists when looking at the provision and continuity provided for special needs children when they move from a sheltered institution into the world of work. In recent years, partly as a result of policies of integration but also because of heightened awareness, much has been done in non-special schools and colleges to accomodate children with physical difficulties in the form of improvements to buildings and facilities – for example, to allow for wheelchairs. Sometimes classes have even been moved into different rooms to avoid precluding the physically handicapped. There are still too many schools, nevertheless, with the will to integrate the special needs pupil but without adequate facilities to do so.

Implicit for pupils with special needs, as for all children, is the need for clear written records and profiles to accompany them on their transfer from one phase to the next. Parents need to be fully involved and conversant with the content of these records at all times. (What can appear trivial in normal circumstances can represent a major achievement for a disadvantaged child.) There needs to be considerably more in-service training provided for teachers in this area, particularly as attitudes and opportunities are constantly changing to incorporate the special needs child into the normal school system. A classic example is the sophistication of hearing-aids and the early stage at which hearing impairment can now be diagnosed. Not only has this meant wider learning opportunities for the child, but also new experiences for the teacher who may be faced with unanticipated problems in teaching the child in a 'normal' class.

Multicultural teaching

This issue is an ever changing one and causes significant difficulties in some areas of the UK. It is likely that more and more teachers will be required to teach classes containing children from a variety of cultures who may speak different languages and have different religious beliefs; they should be aware of and ready to cope with the problems they might meet.

In a rapidly changing society consideration and concern must be shown for *all* children within the confines of our educational system. Some pupils – such as those for whom English is a second language – will require special provision, even if only for a short time, to enable them to succeed and integrate into the mainstream of the education system.

Educationalists at all levels share a commitment to provide for all aspects of our multicultural society; schools formulating whole school policies for curriculum development are well aware of this element.

In the early years the involvement of parents and provision of the bilingual learning requirements of some ethnic minority groups are crucial. It is necessary slowly to break down the many barriers which may inhibit parents from such backgrounds from allowing their children to attend playgroups and nursery schools – particularly where the children come from mixed backgrounds. Many good practices involve parents and community agencies in the learning processes. The major obstacle is to include parents who, for a variety of reasons, find it difficult to take part in their child's early years of educational experience at institutions of all kinds and during the different phases of education. This is most pronounced where the child may have to learn English as a second language – such a child is, clearly, at an initial disadvantage which may not be easily understood by the parent. Often a school will provide a range of activities in order to gain support from the multiethnic community it serves, and to try to bridge the sometimes very wide social gap which can exist between home and school (see Chapter 6).

Such problems can be very pronounced where various forms of assessment tests are used. Most assessors are aware of the language difficulties of children undergoing such tests, but it can be quite difficult to see the cultural biases which are built into many structures. To be consistent with the equality of opportunity philosophy, the measures and norms used must be appropriate to all; this can be singularly difficult to put into practice in multicultural situations.

Racist issues are continually highlighted. Those which affect the children and parents at a local level are perhaps better tackled in the primary stage. It is in this phase of education that many of a child's long-term moral and social values are formed, an understanding of cultural differences can be established and a good start can be made on minimizing the likelihood of prejudice. The secondary school has a far harder task because of the scale and complexity of its organization and administration, the wider catchment areas it draws on, and the constraints in the development of consensus about its aims. There is a need to develop a coherent approach so that all departments of the school are fully conversant with and committed to the policies of the school and the support needed. The transfer from the primary phase to the secondary phase can be especially traumatic for the child who still has culturally based learning problems and needs careful handling by both schools – the parents should be actively involved and comprehensive and accurate records should be used.

Commitment from the head teacher is crucial, as in all areas of development. While some schools' policies stress multicultural curriculum development, others have taken a more directly anti-racist stance. Often parents and community leaders are directly involved in forming the policy and in the design of the curriculum, especially in the role of translators and educators regarding their particular cultural needs. 'Valuing the community languages and the mother tongues of bilingual students is crucial for all schools and multiethnic communities' (Straker-Welds, 1984).

In addition to human resources both within and outside the school, it is important to provide various facilities such as library books, television and video, bilingual packs and special courses. These need to be carefully researched making sure that they reflect the attitudes of the individual provider, other members of the school and the community. Even reading schemes may sometimes present unexpected bias or racist connotations. A strong thread of continuity must be a common concern of educationalists at all levels and in other sectors of the community if racial prejudice and barriers are to be eradicated from the learning and transitional process. By promoting positive attitudes towards the needs of all who make up the community from the earliest years through to adulthood, Straker-Welds (1984) concluded that:

> The development of anti-racist whole school policies at the primary and secondary levels is a step forward in the idea that schools can have corporate aims and as a result carry forward collective reforms across the curriculum.

Community involvement

Pupils need to have an awareness of the wider world, outside the school and home, in which they live and their parents work. Their degree of understanding and involvement will vary according to their age and stage of development and the exposure they get to outside experiences. The media, particularly in the form of television, has done much to widen horizons but tends to provide a somewhat narrow and colourful view of events and situations. Whether as a child or an adult there can be no substitute for personal involvement and experience to put things into their real perspective. Much has been started to improve the awareness of children of the community in which they live and it is encouraging to note that the developments already taking place will aid children in their later transitions through the educational system. A significant factor here is teachers' growing awareness of the commercial and industrial sectors. This is shown by the wider opportunities which have been established for business secondments as a facet of in-service training avenues by the DES.

Many organizations both large and small are keen to become involved with schools at all levels and devote time and resources to ensuring that this happens; for example, many companies now produce very high quality video programmes on free loan to schools and colleges on a wide range of topics, most of which are no longer merely 'company advertising programmes' as they were at one time.

In particular, the library services and 'teachers centres' in most local authorities provide an excellent link by providing a vast range of books, video tapes and other resources covering most local, public and commercial activities. Great care is taken by the staff involved to ensure that the right materials are available to match the pupils' age, stage of development and interest; with written material readableness is a prime criteria in the choice of new materials to stock. Some librarians now link schools with the town library by reading and telling stories in both places. Pupils are often taken to the local library to meet the librarian and staff and to gain an insight into the library system and the facilities available. Parents are also encouraged to take part in this especially when their children are at a very early age.

In some areas the police force is devoting considerable time to becoming involved with schools, both on a formal and informal basis. The Thames Valley police force, like many others, has devised a 'schools programme' and appointed 'community police officers', part of whose duty is regularly to go into schools at all levels. The programme is aimed at helping pupils to become good and responsible citizens and includes safety education, crime prevention and discussion periods on topics proposed by the pupils. The programme is aimed at providing opportunities for the local officers to establish a healthy relationship with the children living in their area. The programme was designed jointly by the Thames Valley Police and the appropriate educationalists and advisers, and is seen as a team effort. The relationships that have been established between the local officer and the class teacher reinforce this professional relationship. Pupils get to know the police officers in their area and, by seeing them regularly throughout their schooling, potential barriers are broken down and a continual relationship is established. Often police officers become involved in less formal ways, for example in helping with sport or extra-curricular school activities.

The police have paid particular attention to their image, but it is equally true that many other people in the community and in specific service sectors are becoming increasingly aware of the benefits of involving themselves with schools and colleges. In particular, involvement with the health service and the fire services is common in many areas.

More schools and colleges are realizing the need to 'market' their establishments positively to their local community so as to achieve the right relationship and degree of involvement. A number of initiatives have been started to introduce the 'marketing' ethos across school and college activities, particularly in the secondary and FE sectors.

Business links

There are many forms of business links with schools and colleges, some of them of very long standing. Recently there has been a greater emphasis on the need for commercial, industrial and professional organizations to become more closely involved with the educational system. Some of this has arisen because of a realization of the benefits of involving business with school, but more is probably due to businesses wanting to make pupils aware at an early age of their needs and the opportunities they offer.

Traditionally, most school governing bodies have some local representation from local businesses, particularly in the secondary and FE sectors, and most establishments have set up various forms of 'steering committees' to ensure that subject content and methods taught relate to the commercial needs. There has been a much greater emphasis in this direction on the examining bodies, particularly those specializing in vocational subjects.

There are many competitions sponsored by business and professional institutions, again mainly aimed at the secondary sector, such as the British Institute of Management's annual national Business Game competition. The Confederation of British Industry (CBI) has many local liaison groups operating, dedicated to following through and encouraging liaison between schools and its member companies. It has established a National Education and Training Committee with the following terms of reference: 'To keep under review all matters to do with education and training as they affect industry and commerce and to take any necessary actions'. Reporting to this committee are a number of panels, in particular the Joint CBI/Schools Panel which has the more specific terms of reference: 'To keep under review questions of common interest and concern to schools and industry and to *assist closer co-operation*'.

Many other initiatives are being established, such as the Department of Trade and Industry (DTI) Enterprise Scheme. Despite industry's natural interest in the secondary sector, much good work is taking place at primary level. For example, a Hertfordshire primary school that was studying machines visited a factory making lawn mowers. The children noticed the amount of oil on the employees' overalls and after discussion were given the problem of how best to remove the oil. They set up various tests and the results were fed back. Another impressive observation made by the children was how well the work force operated as a team. The factory staff gained an understanding of the skills required in discussing their work with the children and realized that the children were able to understand their explanations. Many such examples are developing. The long-term benefits for both parties are not difficult to project. There are many joint co-operative projects between industry and secondary schools, often involving the loan or use of highly sophisticated technology and associated research work. Particular emphasis is currently on encouraging pupils to become aware of the possibilities associated with information technology. Individually, the growth of schemes such as CPVE which necessitate industrial or commercial attachments to gain work experience, are significantly broadening the partnership between schools and industry. Small business enterprises are often set up in schools and are monitored by staff but also assisted by outside business advisers when help is needed. An example is where the pupils run their own 'tuck shop' to the extent that they do their own buying, pricing, accounting and banking. A popular theme is for pupils to raise charity money using their own initiatives.

Last, but by no means least, is the reverse move whereby commercial organizations are beginning to realize that they lack sufficient knowledge of the school system and its attitudes and are either seconding staff to or exchanging them with schools. Commercially this must be of value since it will provide commercial companies with better knowledge of their potential employees or customers of the future. An example of an organization operating this type of scheme is Marks and Spencer.

All these ventures are valuable links in the continuity chain – in these cases going right through to employment.

CHAPTER 6
WHAT DO WE MEAN BY 'GOOD PRACTICE'?

The express purpose of this chapter is to stimulate the reader's own thinking. Examples are described in the context of their original settings, for instance, from the infant/junior sector; nevertheless, with very little imagination the concepts can often be developed for a totally different setting.

As stated, there are many examples of 'good practice' going on at all stages of the educational process and in many areas – some of these are 'unsung' and many of them are not new. They are often regarded by their advocates as 'commonsense' practices and form such an integral part of their philosophy that they would be surprised if anyone suggested that what they were doing was not normal practice. Obviously there is a great deal of room for improvement in the field of transition and continuity. Among those who are currently using and develop ing ideas to further these ends, the schools and the LEAs, in particular, have the nucleus of success from which they can develop their ideas. Essentially, all good practice in transition can only be based on building good relationships with all concerned in a stimulating and satisfying environment. In all transition practices there must be threads of continuity in designing methods and curriculae so that what follows develops from previous experiences.

It would be impossible to cover examples of every practice currently being developed; what the following examples attempt to do is to describe a few successes which are readily transferable in concept and which may stimulate the readers to explore their own ideas further.

Examples from early years

Leaving home and starting school at ages 3–5 years needs much time and effort to be spent by parents and teachers in helping the

WHAT DO WE MEAN BY EXAMPLES OF GOOD PRACTICE?

child to become familiar with the changes in its environment based on its understanding of the home and on previous experiences. Much of this has already been discussed in detail in Chapter 1, and all the good practices here revolve around the methods used in order to gain the involvement and understanding of the parents.

Since the range of options open to children prior to the age of five years are so wide and tend to be very dependent on the cultural and social background of the community, the following represents a 'listing' of some of the most effective practices:

1. Visits to parents in their own homes.
2. Parents initially visiting with their child, but not leaving the child or staying long.
3. Including parents in educational discussions.
4. Organizing celebrations, workshops, etc with parents' help.
5. Community ventures, etc.

With a little imagination the list can be endless.

COMMUNITY LINKS AND THE MULTI-ETHNIC NURSERY

The aim of this school is to be a community-based nursery, both gaining from and giving to the rich and varied area surrounding the school. It is a 70-place nursery set in a densely populated city area which comprises a broad mix of people from a very wide range of ethnic and cultural backgrounds. Members of the local community are welcomed into the school at any time, whether to help, tell a story, cook, bring a newly arrived relative from interesting places such as India, Pakistan, Glasgow or Southend, show off a new baby, drink a cup of tea, play with the children, join in one of the many festival celebrations or just watch.

Admissions

When parents arrive to enrol their child on the waiting list, one of the first questions generally asked is, 'What language do you speak at home?' The next question is, 'Does your child speak that language well?' The teacher makes a point of not asking 'Does your child speak English?' as that can easily be found out when the child is admitted while not disparaging the child's fluency in his or her own mother tongue. Two members of the staff are Sikh and can help all the staff to discover whether the children have a grasp of basic concepts when their own language is used; the staff can all use a little Punjabi, Urdu or Hindi which is a link with many new children. Visits to the childrens' homes are carried out informally for many reasons; the staff are always welcomed and gain a great deal on such occasions. The key to these visits and all relationships is *acceptance* not judgement.

Involvement

Child-minders are welcome to the school as well as parents, aunties, uncles, grandparents and neighbours, together with the younger children and babies they cared for.

Classes in English are held from time to time, whenever there is a demand and a teacher is available, usually coming from the Industrial Language Centre. Craft classes are held weekly run by an instructor; mothers are encouraged to participate in learning a new craft or sharing their own skills with others. They often make gifts for their own families or to give to the school, but more importantly, they enjoy each other's company, even though eight members in a group might speak eight different languages, originate from different countries and have varied cultures and educational experiences themselves!

Films and talks are given most weeks for parents or other interested people. These are usually in English or Punjabi, but someone is on hand to interpret languages if necessary. The topics cover such areas as: the dangers of fire, prevention of rickets, using library books, home safety, road safety, going to 'first' school, helping your child at home, places to go in the school holidays, a good diet for pre-school children.

Activities

Outings: Parents, relations and friends are welcome to join in with the school outings. Children are frequently taken out in small groups to widen their experiences; visits to a farm, a cattle market, a stately home, the bank, the post office, the park and many other places can be arranged. Two main outings are organized each year for the whole family. One is on a weekday to a place such as Whipsnade Zoo; two coaches usually go on this trip. The second is usually on a Saturday in early July to the seaside; six coaches are usually needed for this outing. In this case everyone's friends and relations are invited, with ages ranging from six weeks to over eighty. This outing means that many fathers have a chance to join in and share their children's experiences. Staff willingly give their time to such (ad)ventures.

Festivals: The aim here is to share with the children specific festivals that would normally be celebrated at home, consequently learning more about the range of cultures; this develops mutual respect, tolerance and understanding at the same time as providing pleasurable experiences.

Swimming: Groups of children are taken to the nearby swimming pool. Mothers, toddlers and babies and others who wish to go are invited; they wear swimsuits or other forms of clothing depending on the requirements of their culture.

Library

With the help and advice of the Schools Library Service, a well-stocked library has been established. Books are taken home by the children. With the help of parents, children can change their books at the beginning or end of each nursery session. Books are available in many different languages and adults are asked to share them with their children. Fostering an interest in books will stand them in good stead throughout the rest of their education and lives.

Benefits

There are many obvious and lasting benefits from community nursery involvement. The many volunteers who are encouraged to come into the school from the local community, whatever the language they speak most fluently, all prove invaluable to the nursery.

Children become much more confident at an early age when they are able to use their mother tongue to converse with adults about their activities and experiences. Their English develops more quickly and they readily become bilingual, never confusing one language with another, even at pre-school age. The transfer of these children to the next stage is far smoother.

An extended days and terms scheme has been introduced as a result of the enthusiasm of the community.

TRANSITION AND THE NURSERY SCHOOL

This relates to the approach and philosophy of a 70-place nursery school set in a country town in which all under-fives have access to nursery provision. The children generally spend up to a year at the nursery. Most of the children transfer to the town's large 350-place primary school, the remainder to one of the nearby small rural primary schools. The large primary school is geographically and administratively totally separate.

General approach

Everything the children do in the nursery is planned so as to build confident, happy children with enquiring minds, which prepares children effectively for the transition to the next school. Activities are structured throughout the year so that the children become used to conforming to both large and small group activities. Quite a lot of pre-reading, writing and mathematical work is done with the rising-five age group – about one hour per day at this stage. The children do movement and drama, a lot of singing and listening to tapes, etc, having reached the stage of being able to thoroughly enjoy such experiences. This is also a very good way of preparing children for the infant classes of the next school. Perhaps most important of all, is the strong emphasis on a considerable amount of 'socializing', which will help the child to become a confident member of any group. Differences in personal characteristics are encouraged and appreciated; it is interesting to observe children's personalities through the way they interact with one another.

The primary connection
The rising five-year-olds are taken for three or four long visits to the primary school. The teacher accompanies them and spends time there, often teaching children who originally attended the infant school, while the infants attend their classes. The infants enjoy these visits and some cannot wait to join the school during their last few weeks of nursery school.

Parents
Parents are encouraged into the school as friends at all times. There are various regular meetings throughout the year, for example of new parents, governors and other interested people, and many of these meetings will continue in the schools to which they transfer. The parents' attendance at the nursery school is very high, but sadly drops off as the children move on.

'Work evenings', where parents go to the school and help in various tasks, have been deliberately chosen to extend and build up friendships. These enable even stronger relationships to become established with the parents; often both personal and general concerns are discussed and the time to meet parents without the presence of the children is valued. As the third-term approaches the topic of 'going to the big school' becomes important and often the staff feel that they have been helpful by just 'talking it through'.

Staff
Staff training days have been spent sharing experiences with other teachers. In particular, about 50 per cent of the time has been spent with the staff of the large primary school. Records have

been jointly developed which are acceptable to both schools. The headteacher of the infant school also keeps in close touch with the headteachers of the other eight small primary schools which the nursery feeds.

INFANT TO JUNIOR

This example involves two schools which, although completely autonomous and in separate buildings, are situated on the same campus, although the playgrounds are separated by a large grass expanse. The infant school has 200 pupils and the junior 250. Transfer normally takes place at the age of seven years.

Prior to an initiative by the two heads which resulted from an in-service training activity, the infants visited the junior school in the last term before transition. They also occasionally joined together for entertainment and 'theatre-type trips'.

Since this, the degree of interface has escalated considerably and takes place on a more planned and regular basis. Among the new main links are:

— Children visit each other's establishments to make better use of facilities such as physical exercise equipment.
— Some first- and second-year juniors visit the infants at playtimes to renew friendships and answer questions.
— Joint activities are specifically arranged, for example the older children write stories for the infants and involve them in the development of the stories.
— Teachers are now scheduled to spend time in each other's classrooms and to discuss issues involving curriculum continuity.
— Joint agreement has been reached by consensus over effective record keeping and transfer documentation, and is regularly kept under review.
— Consultation over new policies and curriculum schemes now automatically takes place.
— Each school now becomes involved in the other's 'celebrations'.

Essentially, the staff have helped the two headteachers to build two well-integrated teams.

'Within school' practices

This example started in response to a particular LEA's policy to integrate, as far as possible, children with special needs into mainstream educational provision. This gave rise to many new issues concerning the head and staff which then made them take a wider look at their existing policies and systems. After all, nearly all children have some 'special needs' at some time or other, the only difference is that with a few children this has been identified 'officially'.

This is a junior school catering for 220 children whose age range is from 7–11 years. It is set in an urban conurbation. The description which follows is in the original 'special needs' context.

Records
Initially, the key problem was seen as ensuring that there was complete accord in, and understanding of, the record base which could be pertinent to the child's needs, and that any alert to a potential problem was picked up. The following is a list of possible sources of such information:

— Teacher and Support Services developmental records.
— Language monitoring documents.
— Reports from Language Centres.
— Reports from Adjustment Centres.
— Documents for Statemented children.
— Relevant letters from parents.
— Notes from headteachers and teachers.
— Reports from psychologists.
— Reports from doctors and nurses.
— Developmental records for the visually, hearing or physically impaired.
— Curricular development records.
— Test results for language, mathematics, reading, etc.
— Internal confidential records devised by the school.

These apply, together with any other relevant material.

Briefing and discussion sessions
The staff meet on a regular basis – at least termly – to introduce children to colleagues using the LEA's pupil record and photograph. After disseminating information and an outline of possible strategies for managing the child's progress (as has been developed by the teacher), if this has already been determined, a general discussion takes place to agree collective staff action regarding the child. New children joining in the middle of a term are introduced as part of the regular staff 'organizational' meet-

ings. It is important that *all* staff are fully aware of *all* children, the appropriate strategies which have been devised and the need to take collective responsibility.

Classes
All staff spend time, on a regular basis, taking each other's classes in order to get to know the children. This can be for quite a short period, for example, a 'story time' of 20–30 minutes.

Handling needs or problems
As a result of the preceding steps, children's needs can be catered for and an awareness of specific difficulties will be produced which will lead to practical and moral support for the teachers directly responsible from their colleagues.

Monitoring
There are regular review discussions – these are inter-class and inter-school (involving transfer schools) – on curricular work and what has been done and will be done with a view to ensuring positive progress. Special attention is paid to continuity and the avoidance of unnecessary repetition.

Primary/secondary liaison

The six case histories which follow are very diverse in their approach and have been chosen because of the ease with which the lessons contained can be applied to other situations.

A PROJECT ON PRIMARY/SECONDARY LIAISON
Introduction
This first example started some 10 years ago as an initiative between the primary schools which fed a specific secondary school. Often, approaches depend on the commitment of one or two people for their continuance, so it is important to emphasize that while there have inevitably been many changes in staff, particularly of headteachers, and there have been 'ups and downs', this project is still going strong.

Background
The schools involved in this project were: a comprehensive school with approximately 510 pupils whose ages ranged from 11 to 16 years; ten, mainly rural, primary schools who acted as feeder schools and ranged in size from 23 to 130 pupils. These had formed into a 'federation' of small schools in 1978. The original headteachers in the 'federation' had been meeting regularly for some

time when the new appointment was made of a headteacher in the comprehensive school. It was decided that the head be invited to join the federation, which he willingly did.

The LEA became involved as a result of well-argued requests for funding and the deep interest of its advisory service in what it saw as a constructive and worthwhile innovation in the authority.

Liaison

This developed from one visit by junior children (from the primary schools) to the comprehensive and by the head of that school's first year to each of the feeder primary schools in the summer term, into a wide variety of activities:

- a) Headteacher meetings termly which also involved the appropriate primary and secondary advisers from the LEA.
- b) Pupils visited the comprehensive schools regularly throughout their junior years for sport and music/drama productions, etc.
- c) Fourth-year juniors had swimming and musical instrument lessons via the comprehensive.
- d) Parents of fourth-year pupils at the primary schools were invited to the comprehensive school for various functions and to an information 'observation' day.
- e) Staff were encouraged to meet informally for social activities.
- f) Pupils, parents and staff of all the schools were involved in musical productions.

Continuity

- a) Records are passed on, considerable discussion is taking place on what is needed and modifications are being made; this is an area where it is agreed that still more can be done.
- b) Reports on first-year comprehensive children were returned to their feeding primary schools for comments from their former teachers.
- c) The head of the first year from the comprehensive still visits each primary school in the summer term to establish contact with the children, not just the teachers.
- d) Loans of musical and science equipment, together with instrumental tuition, were arranged by the comprehensive school for all junior pupils.
- e) An industrial and school relations project on craft, design

and technology (CDT) was established involving both primary and secondary pupils.

f) A weekend conference on curriculum for both primary and secondary staff was organized and funded by the LEA.

Working parties were established and reports written, the outcomes providing guidelines for further discussion.

Evaluation of joint conference

Teacher attitudes to their colleagues in other sectors were originally not conducive to continuity; a lot more preparation was required in promoting understanding of each other's phase and how they fitted into the total process. Primary school staff were very protective of their breadth and child-centred approach, while secondary school staff found it difficult to see their subject specialisms 'dissected'! They all felt gratified to see how discussion broke down these barriers and how guidelines for small group discussions were produced.

It was surprising to note the disparity between expectations and curriculum content in many areas between the individual primary schools. Much more understanding needed promoting through inter-school visits.

Presentation of work caused less of a threat to teachers as this was seen to be an area where in-service training could help ensure continuity. Different departments in the secondary school had not realized the conflicting demands they made on children in this area.

Tremendous strides forwards were made by the staff meeting one another on neutral territory and in an informal setting – they got to know each other and were able to make firm contacts.

Long-term concerns

These were that:

a) Momentum would be hard to maintain because of the day-to-day pressures on staff.
b) Changes of staff, especially heads, caused some disruption and a need to re-establish commitments.
c) A third-party, namely the LEA advisory service, needed to act as a catalyst.

Project benefits

The whole project had been of considerable value to the pupils, parents and staff during this potentially traumatic transition process, for example:

— Pupils became familiar with some of the staff, buildings and aspects of the organization before entry day.
— Parents had plenty of opportunity to gain insight into and become familiar with routines and procedures before their children transferred.
— Staff were gaining a better understanding of both the benefits and constraints of each other's work.

Conclusion
Projects like this are beginning to produce effective results and much effort and commitment is needed by all concerned to keep the momentum going. The LEA has encouraged, however, other primary/secondary groupings to form and follow similar aims and objectives. It is significant, even in this fairly close-knit example, that the time scales for real benefit are long since changes in attitudes are essentially a very slow process.

By means of the grant-related in-service training (GRIST) fund, considerable progress is being made in the primary secondary interface in the area of the mathematics curriculum. Comprehensive schools are currently moving towards a co-ordinated first-year curriculum and promoting their pupils' understanding of the relevance of their studies to their environment and community. Staff are being given the appropriate opportunities to develop teaching strategies appropriate to 'active' learning methods.

LAUNCHING PRIMARY AND SECONDARY LIAISON

In this case the emphasis started with a belief and commitment in the LEA that far more should and could be done to smooth the transition of children from primary to secondary schools. To do this it established an in-service training course specifically on the subject of this liaison.

Course participants
Applicants for this course had to be in groups of four, each of which comprised two secondary and two primary teachers working in the same catchment area. Each group had to involve a teacher from the secondary school with responsibility for first-year pupils and include a primary head. In preparation for the course the group had to negotiate a commitment as to the outcome of the course with their in-service consortium, to ensure that follow-up work from the course would take place.

WHAT DO WE MEAN BY EXAMPLES OF GOOD PRACTICE?

Course structure
The course was residential and lasted three days, during which some of the problems of primary and secondary school liaison were explored resulting in a better definition of the roles and responsibilities of the first-year tutor and form tutor in secondary schools.

Opportunities were provided for the primary school teachers to gain more insight into the organization of secondary schools and similarly for the secondary school teachers to look at primary school situations. Teachers were helped to develop some skills in the clearer analysis of observable classroom situations. One of the three days was mainly spent visiting each other's sector, allowing for one secondary school teacher and two primary school teachers to be in the same classroom carrying out observations and then comparing findings.

The final element in the three days focused on developing action plans at an individual level, at a group level and, by no means least, at a catchment area level. This last set of plans would mean further negotiations outside the immediate context of the course.

Outcomes
The targets set by the individuals suggest that, if good intentions lead to action, some worthwhile programme of initiatives would emerge, such as for example:

— There would be a review of records carried out in a catchment area.
— Regular visits to each other's classrooms would take place in future.
— Use would be made of in-service training opportunities to investigate particular issues.
— There would be a re-examination of the attitudes towards homework.
— Mutually agreed curricula would be developed for subject areas such as science.

With the individual inspectors and advisers who have responsibility for the participating schools being involved in the planning of the sessions, it is anticipated that there will be support and encouragement for such outcomes.

A CROSS-CURRICULAR APPROACH
This project is in its early stages and involves a town comprehensive school of over 700 pupils and its five main feeder schools of between 150 and 250 pupils.

Prior to 1985 when the current comprehensive headteacher was appointed, liaison was very low key and familiarization visits for the pupils were the sum total of activity. Progress since then has been rapid and far more liaison now takes place for both pupils and staff. In particular, curriculum continuity in the mathematics area is being established and continually developed with the aid of GRIST funding, which started in 1987.

Plans are being implemented to develop cross-curriculum projects in the lower school using an 'action research' methodology to:

a) develop a problem-solving approach to learning, with special emphasis on the environmental theme;
b) improve the academic and social induction of pupils at the age of 11 years; and
c) investigate the use of materials which will be used in the primary schools with a view to subsequent development in the comprehensive school.

These plans are continually being refined based on the experiences being gained.

This project involves collaboration, rather than just liaison, between primary and comprehensive teaching staff, and the development of cross-curricular projects across all departments in the comprehensive. The intended outcome of the plan, which is not expected to come to full fruition until 1989, are:

a) changed styles of learning and teaching methods within the relevant departments;
b) increased cross-curricular work in the first and second year in the comprehensive;
c) production of integrated curricular materials;
d) development of a coherent programme for pupils from the ages of 10–13 years which can be followed through in the lower school as a whole.

The benefits of the closer co-operation of all those involved are already being felt.

OAKS FROM ACORNS!

This example shows what can develop when two enthusiastic members of staff get together through their own volition to tackle the continuity issue.

The secondary school in this example is again run as a comprehensive, but with an age range of 11 – 18 years and nearly 1,300 pupils from a predominantly suburban area. In this case the start was made with just one of the feeder schools of 230 children and is being gradually extended.

The start
In 1986/7 the head of the history department in the comprehensive and the deputy head of one of the larger feeder junior schools decided to try and look at how the two schools could work better together as a result of a planned junior school journey in which the head of history had become involved. They planned to work alongside each other in each other's sectors on a half-day per week release basis which was wholeheartedly supported by their respective headteachers. The aim was to develop a common skills-based curriculum in history using the local environment during the last year of the junior school and the first year of the secondary. Evaluation of this first partnership showed a tremendous gain in continuity for the pupils who were transferring and in the development of the teachers' understanding of each other's work and constraints.

The continuation
In order to continue, develop and extend this work, supply cover was obtained via GRIST funding in 1987/8 and tremendous advances were made.

Parents, school governors and others were invited to attend exhibitions of the children's work from the two schools and the two key members of staff involved have given much time to in-service training activities in both their own LEA and elsewhere. Materials have been produced and considerable interest is being shown in this project nationally. (Materials are being jointly published by the two staff involved.)

The extension
Plans for 1988/9 have already been made and are being implemented. These plans will continue the development of a skills-based history curriculum for the ages of 9 – 13 years. Another large primary school is now involved and the project will be developed to extend the skills-based aspect of the work to the development of cross-curricular assessment in the two primary schools. A further development will be an agreed monitoring system for cross-curricular skills relating to project work and history at the comprehensive school.

An urban experience in a deprived area

This case is an example of a particular response to a specific educational challenge.

Background

This is a large comprehensive in a poor and socially deprived large urban inner city area.

Due to falling rolls it was under threat of closure for four years. As was expected, parents in the catchment area who were concerned and able chose not to send their children to the school. Consequently, in the latter two or three years only children from very poor and unmotivated environments attended the school and in falling numbers.

Action

It seemed to the headteacher and the staff pointless to continue an 'O' level examination-orientated curriculum as it was completely beyond their pupils' ability. With the help of outside supporting agencies, a complete review of the curriculum was made. The purpose was to base the curriculum on the needs of the children at the school and to maintain motivation.

Staff had to adapt and learn how to teach other subjects other then their own specialisms. The curriculum had to have breadth and be relevant; this took much staff time in both discussion and in-service training.

Results

Not an easy task, but it had tremendous compensations. The pupils were less disruptive and to a certain degree took interest in most areas.

Parents seemed pleased by the results to the extent that they were prepared to show interest. The staff, if reluctant at first, conquered their initial misgivings and now actually enjoy the variety of work embraced in their teaching. They found more time for individual pupils, the benefits of which cannot be overemphasized and do not need expansion here.

Moral

Surely this must bring into stark relief the need to design student-centred rather than subject-centred educational programmes. These programmes must take into account the needs of the community and the flexibility which teachers will have to develop. Moreover, it illustrates well the constructive effect that an appropriate curriculum can have on attitudes and behaviour patterns.

WHAT DO WE MEAN BY EXAMPLES OF GOOD PRACTICE?

FALLING ROLL OPPORTUNISM!

As a result of the falling numbers in the secondary sector of education, it was suggested by the headteacher of a primary school that the space now available in the local secondary school could be used as a classroom for primary school children.

Creating the ethos

After much discussion in which the LEA became involved, a domestic science area was adapted, refurbished and turned into a primary classroom facility. Teachers of the fourth-year primary pupils were involved in setting the room up with the appropriate materials and displays to create the right ethos for the primary children to work in.

It was decided that the room would be available throughout the pupils' last year in the primary sector. Feeder schools would have the opportunity to work there for a period of time on a rota basis.

Outcomes

Originally the aims of the project were primarily to familiarize children with the building and organization of the secondary school they were to join shortly. As will be seen, the benefits are much wider than this.

While primary teachers accompanied their pupils to the 'new' classroom, secondary teachers were invited to contribute their particular specialisms where appropriate and took the opportunity to do so. Older pupils in the secondary school took an interest and became involved with the primary classes in a variety of ways. The following are some of the many benefits to the primary children:

— They became used to the geography of the building and the people in it.
— The ideas of specific 'subject' timetables and homework were discussed.
— Better PE facilities were offered.

The staff gained a far better insight into each other's worlds than was possible just from visiting and discussion.

Extension

The success of this first project has led to the development of more 'in secondary' primary classrooms being established as space becomes available in secondary schools. Where this has not been possible additional units have been added to the sites of comprehensive schools, where appropriate, and set up as primary bases.

The use of grounds has also been developed by a 'primary coordinator' of a group of primary schools in some areas, and secondary school pupils are working alongside those from the primary school sector in creating wild areas and ponds for joint study purposes.

Examples of multi-school approaches, federations and consortia

Over the past few years many educational establishments, ranging from infant to further education, have formed themselves into groups as a result of a mutually agreed need to do so or of an initiative from the LEA. Some of these arrangements have been catalysed (as in the schools/FE clusters described on page 97) by a significant change which has resulted in a major rethinking of approaches to areas of curriculum.

Such groupings are variously called 'pyramids', 'federations', 'clusters', 'consortia', etc. I find it difficult to distinguish between these and feel that the label chosen is largely a result of what is favoured by the relevant sector or authority rather than having any deep seated significance. There is little doubt, however, that the trend towards close groupings is a good move in the direction of effective transition and continuity.

FEDERATIONS

One example of a 'federation' has already been quoted on page 86 in some detail. This had its early roots in getting together a few small schools, which coincidentally happened to feed a particular secondary school, to form a 'federation'. Here the initial impetus was the need to share views and develop ideas on teaching and administrative problems, and early on the group sought the help of the LEA advisory service. The involvement of the secondary school came later. This concept – which involves primary and secondary schools, both together and separately – has been extended with the help of the LEA to form a number of other federations, clusters or consortia. All of these tend to have slightly different 'membership' parameters but adopt the same general principles regarding common areas of mutual interest and benefit.

PYRAMIDS

Some LEAs have formed their schools into pyramid structures –

WHAT DO WE MEAN BY EXAMPLES OF GOOD PRACTICE?

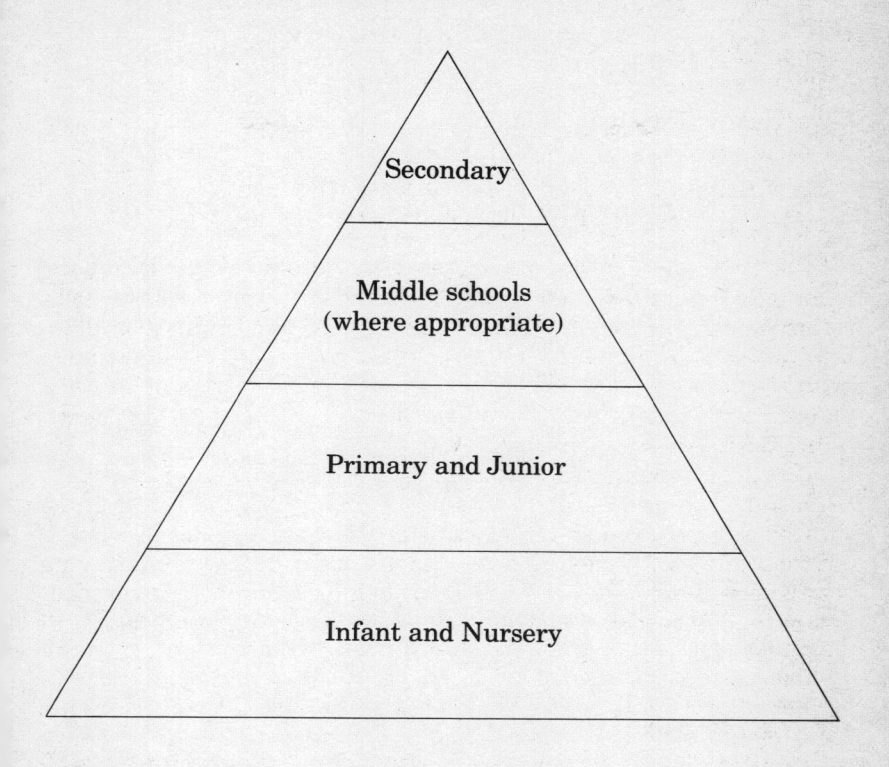

```
              /\
             /  \
            /Secondary\
           /----------\
          / Middle schools \
         / (where appropriate) \
        /----------------------\
       /   Primary and Junior   \
      /--------------------------\
     /      Infant and Nursery    \
    /_____\
```

Figure 1. LEA pyramid structure for schools

where geographically possible, within catchment areas — as the diagram shows.

The main theme of this is to arrange a series of regular scheduled meetings involving all levels of staff, although not often all at once. There are various agreed agendas, for example, some of the meetings have a particular subject orientation. Most result in agreement of a specific action, which is subsequently followed up.

The logistics of meetings are fairly apparent, there being two main types: lateral across a particular level of the pyramid and vertical.

As a result of this approach there has been a vast improvement in the quality of transfer information, which has resulted in:

— increased primary and secondary liaison, both formal through the system and informal;

— greater awareness of teaching ethos and curriculum content;
— structured pupil inductions at all levels;
— greater parental involvement.

Quotations from two members of pyramids summarize well the general results accruing from this particular approach:

a) from the teacher of a secondary school,

> They intend to introduce a system which transferred the experience and practice of the primary sector, into the early years of the secondary sector using the added departmental expertise which they had gained.

b) from a primary headteacher in a pyramid group,

> The aim in the first instance is not necessarily curriculum continuity or pastoral continuity, but to promote mutual understanding and trust between teachers across the primary/secondary divide.

CONSORTIA AND CLUSTERS

The Technical and Vocational Education Initiative has resulted in a major rethink of the syllabi and curriculum content in many subject areas. In particular in the 16+ subject areas, especially where the orientation is vocational rather than academic. This has meant a close examination and an agreement of the teaching content, resources needed and methods of assessment at all levels. Since the pupils undertaking this path are only just about to pass into the 16+ education opportunities, the involvement of establishments solely teaching at these levels, such as colleges of further education, might well have been seen as an intrusion.

Nationally, this initiative has involved a considerable amount of goodwill and time and effort on behalf of all staff involved. In this case some provision was made for resourcing the preparatory work both by the MSC (now the Training Commission) and LEAs.

The following two examples are quoted from widely separated and very different LEAs.

a) In the first local authority, the secondary establishments throughout the county were grouped together in consortia so that each FE establishment was associated with a specific group of secondary schools and in most cases a 'special' school.

Funding was devolved to each consortium in order that they should work together in determining and establishing how to meet their in-service training needs. The mutual benefits from this approach have resulted in in-service training arrangements which are similar in content and structure across the county and to which all establishments involved are committed.

b) The second authority has taken a slightly different approach, partly because of the differing system of provision at 16+.

Secondary schools were grouped into 'clusters' of about four, based on the geographical proximity of their catchment areas. Within each cluster a number of subject working parties were established to develop common approaches. At least one representative from each cluster regularly met with representatives of other clusters to compare progress and agree how differences should be resolved. Each cluster has an FE representative attached to it to ensure subsequent subject continuity or entry acceptability for other courses of study; this means that the same FE representative may have to attend more than one cluster meeting.

The system is working well although the time needed is greater than was originally anticipated. The exchange of teaching ideas and continuity has, naturally, spilled over into many other areas outside the initial TVEI terms of reference. The level of understanding and ongoing informal relationships would probably not have taken place without the impetus of this initiative.

In the case of the FE establishments, the real benefit will probably not be seen until 1988/9 when the first TVEI students will start arriving from the secondary schools.

Careers advice and guidance

Throughout a pupil's education, career information, guidance and choice can sometimes be badly organized. The following is an example of how one LEA defines the operational role of its careers service.

AIMS AND OBJECTIVES

The overall purpose of the service is defined in its aim, which is to help individuals leaving full-time education to make a satisfactory transition from school to college to work. This aim is achieved by:

- acting as a bridge between education, training and employment;
- assisting schools and colleges in forming and implementing a programme of careers education, encouraging its development and providing a positive contribution to the total provision;
- providing a vocational guidance service for all in full-time education;
- providing an information service covering careers, employment, further and higher education for young people, parents, employers and teachers;
- providing a placing service for young people leaving full-time education or youth training schemes and other relevant people who seek to use the careers service;
- helping employers find suitable young employees, and advising them on recruitment and developments in education;
- providing an advisory service for the young unemployed and for those seeking job changes;
- actively participating in youth training and other government schemes to assist young people.

OPERATION
The service is organized to offer advice and guidance in a variety of ways depending on who requests the help, and is very flexible in its approach. Those which are particularly relevant to this book are:

for schools

- by offering advice and support to the school's careers teacher(s) in providing careers education programmes and specific careers information;
- through individual vocational guidance interviews for fifth- and sixth-year pupils and their parents;
- by offering advice to third-year pupils and parents on the options available;
- through the use of a computerized vacancy matching system for those seeking employment or by the YTS route;

— informing teachers about trends and changes in the employment market and continuing education to help them in their tutorial role.

for employers

— by maintaining a computerized vacancy matching system for seeking recruits under the age of 19 years;
— by providing advice on recruitment and training;
— by advising on developments in education;
— by providing information on schemes such as the YTS, which is designed to encourage the employment and training of young people.

In general, the service encourages and advises on the setting up and provision of careers libraries in schools. Each careers office has a well-stocked careers library open to both young people and parents; this includes reference books, prospectuses and a comprehensive range of leaflets and pamphlets. They also prepare specific leaflets on careers and organize careers conventions and conferences for pupils, parents and teachers.

Parental involvement

There are so many diverse examples of parental involvement that only one is mentioned here, which is probably the most outstanding in the world today.

The children's palaces in China have variously been described as pressure establishments and as centres of 'social indoctrination'. Whether this is true or not there is much to learn from them.

These government-funded buildings are to be found in most large towns. They provide a centre which has an enormous range of extra-curricular activities for children outside school hours and at weekends. The activities available range from the arts and sciences through to sporting activities; any child with an interest can become involved and, naturally, particular talents are especially fostered.

The palaces are managed on a voluntary basis and nearly all tuition is provided by dedicated, talented parents. Most significant of all, however, is the degree of parental involvement. Parents accompany their children and also participate in the classes themselves so that they can subsequently help their children at home. The atmosphere is not just one of dedication, but also of the considerable happiness that is gained by all who are involved – children, parents and organizers alike.

The motivation of children in these circumstances is immeasurably enhanced by such parental involvement.

Conclusion
These are just a few examples of what can be considered to be good practice that illustrate the rapid growth that has taken place recently in concern about transition and continuity across the sectors of the educational process. This is very encouraging – it is comforting to know that for many more children the passage will be smoother, although for others there is still room for much improvement. From my experience, the reader may well be surprised at some of the good ideas which are often being adopted in schools nearby; the need is actively to seek out what is happening locally, recognize good practice and adapt ideas to new environments and applications.

CHAPTER 7
SPECIFIC TECHNIQUES

Record-keeping systems

In making sure that the educational process is a continuum, effective record systems are not just desirable but are an essential component. With the current moves in the administration and control of education, it is inevitable that systems could be imposed if adequate approaches do not already exist (GERBIL). Considerable thought must be given to the information which would best accompany the individual child throughout his or her schooling to ensure that continuity in development takes a smooth path. This is true not only within but also between schools; the need should be obvious where the major changes in educational phases take place and are easier to discern when these tend to be curriculum specific. The difficulties of perceiving need seem to arise when the records relate to social development and skills, and where there is 'normal' transfer between teachers within an establishment. If records are to be used in helping one teacher take over where the other left off, they must be accessible and meaningful while remaining factual and objective. These records also need to be kept simple in order to be easily understandable and quick to use, which implies some standardization both in administration and content but still preserves the opportunity to describe individual achievement and needs.

Essentially, records should contain information on what the child or group of children have and have not done, and know and do not yet know. This applies to both curricular and social aspects of their development since one can clearly cause problems in the other area. It also helps if there is information on what has been tried, the degree of success and where specific problems and difficulties have arisen together with possible causes. Teachers can then plan their teaching far more effectively to fulfil children's needs in the light of such knowledge.

It is evident that this information is more available in the early years, since attention to detail of this kind is frequently used.

Later on in the school system, grading approaches seem to be more widely used. The emphasis seems to be on sorting, grouping and classifying children, rather than ensuring that individual children are continuously provided with educational content and stimulus which is matched to their needs.

Where classifications such as grades are used these can be very misleading. What grade 'B' means to one person can be very different to another's interpretation. So-called objective tests, unless extremely carefully constructed and administered, can be very flattering or damaging to a child and usually represent a snapshot in time rather than performance. Certainly some schools are better served by types of 'grading' procedures, providing they have been carefully thought through and the uses agreed between the staff who are going to handle the results.

THE NATURE OF RECORDS

Particular methods of recording information concerning educational progress and performance depend on a variety of factors which will greatly affect their nature and the method of collection and record keeping. The main factors are:

— Why is the record being kept?
— Who is going to use the information and who should have access to it?
— What justification is there for keeping the particular information?
— When is the information going to be referred to and for what reason?
— How long should the information be kept?
— Where should the records be kept?
— Where should the records be stored.

CONFIDENTIALITY

Undoubtedly this is the most sensitive and contentious of all issues where record keeping is concerned.

The purpose of recording and using such potentially sensitive information is the need to provide factual data on which teachers can appropriately and sympathetically base future teaching strategies. Ideally, all such records should be available to the child's parents or guardians. Some information from the records may also need to be made available to other agencies at the discretion of the headteacher, but sometimes subject to directives from their LEA (whether for local or national reasons).

Many of the difficulties regarding the disclosure of information recorded concerning a pupil's performance at school, are related to the differences in perception of the parents' interpretation and misinterpretation of the facts. Others concern the effect that certain information might have on the relationship between parent and child or their ability to interpret the implications correctly.

Such emotive issues cause most teachers to hesitate when recording information that it might be difficult to disclose to parents or guardians. However, if this is a problem, a greater one arises when information becomes available which may affect a child's performance from outside the school system, for example from the social services. Undoubtedly, considerable care and thought must be given to the structure and security of records.

THE USE OF RECORDS

In a project carried out by the National Foundation for Educational Research (NFER) (1978) it was established that teachers felt:

a) if records were 'open' they would no longer be able to pass information on freely and confidentially; consequently, either information would be lost or different channels for passing on the information would be found (eg informally by telephone);
b) being professionals, they should be able to formulate records in a professional and responsible manner;
c) they should be aware of the fact that what they write can have an important effect on the pupil's future;
d) if parents wish to see their child's records then they should be able to do so, providing that this was in the presence of the teacher who could explain and, where necessary, justify what was written;
e) all recording should be totally factual and parents should not only have the right to see this information but also be kept closely informed.

While it is generally felt that records should indeed be 'open', there are perhaps a few occasions where it is necessary and in the best interest of the child that some confidential information should not be formally recorded but should be verbally passed on, for example on their personality or social behaviour.

The difficult problem concerning recorded information is to determine how relevant it is to current situations. An important question which needs to be continually addressed is 'Is the record sufficiently up to date?'; it is all too easy for teachers to come to false conclusions about a child, particularly if the record has preceded their meeting the child and is based on out-of-date information.

Many LEAs have clear policies on the confidentiality and disclosure of the records which accompany children throughout their education. Teachers clearly need to ascertain the precise conditions of their employing authority and abide by them, while adopting approaches which are in the best interests of the child.

The Hampshire Examinations and Assessment Unit based at the University of Southampton, has worked on a 'primary school pupil assessment project' jointly with the Hampshire LEA. The issues raised by this project on the records needed for inter-school transfer are described later in the chapter. Their results can be summarized when discussing the value of records formulated within the pyramidal structure as follows:

> ... there was agreement between all pyramids to distinguish between the short-term needs to assure easy transfer of individual pupils and the longer term initiatives of curriculum content, continuity and teaching methods found within the 5-16 curriculum ...

Assessment and attainment

In the 1960s and early 1970s words like assessment, evaluation and attainment were words seldom heard in the general educational scenario, except in their very general sense or in specific aspects of special educational needs. Curriculum policies and balances were very much regarded as the province of the educational experts; these were in-house matters and there was minimal interference from outside the profession.

This started to change with the formation of the Schools Education Council in 1960, now superseded by the Schools Curriculum Development and Secondary Examination Councils (SCDC and SEC), where 'advice on request' was offered but no teacher needed to act on it; the principle of teacher control at the individual school level was firmly established. Indeed, curriculum policy was kept very low profile, apparently as a minor subset of the broader educational policy. Since then there have been many dramatic changes, particularly over the recent decade, in involvement from outside the profession, not only at local but more significantly now at national levels. One of the major influences has been from the 'Black' papers. These are compilations of critical articles written by generally right-wing educationalists and politicians questioning or attacking various aspects of the British educational system, especially aspects that might broadly be called modern or progressive – for example, discovery learning and continual assessment – and suggesting that academic standards are in decline. The name serves to associate them with, and yet distinguish them from, the government's official policy statements called 'White Papers'. Obviously these 'Black' papers influenced politicians in the Great Debate (1976). Another main national influence is that exerted by the Training Commission as a major client and provider of financial resources, particularly in the later stages of education, such as the Technical and Vocational Education Initiative (TVEI). The major changes of the organization into predominantly comprehensive institutions heralded the change of attitude. The focus of political attention on curriculum matters by the general public has steadily increased since then. The Black papers drew sharp attention to the apparent fall in standards of progressive education and its so-called 'permissive' teaching styles were blamed for this decline. However, this accusation was found to be inappropriate as a result of subsequent research activities. The attention of parents was roused and much publicity was focused on this issue. Curriculum had been thrust into the public domain and the 'Great Debate' of 1976 called for standards to be examined and raised.

The Department of Education and Science invited both industry and the Trades Union Congress (TUC) to participate with educationalists in discussing the need for a national curriculum and the possibility of achieving a consensus on skills, values and attitudes which could be delivered and help pupils to prepare for later life. The Director General of the Confederation of British Industry stressed 'the growing dissatisfaction with standards of achievement in the basic skills reached by many school leavers' (*Times Educational Supplement,* 1976). The formation of the Manpower Services Commission, now renamed the Training Commission was the major government response to the high levels of unemployment among school-leavers and its importance led to a number of specific activities, such as TVEI and the Youth Opportunity Programmes, now the YTS.

All this closer scrutiny of the educational system has inevitably led to a far greater need for accountability by the providers. The distinction between assessment and evaluation is often blurred. In educational terms, assessment means that judgements are made based on information that has been collected by a variety of means concerning the knowledge, skills or attitudes of pupils – the assumption being that it is possible to measure potential success or failure by gauging performance against the achievement of previous targets. We are all continually making judgements about different situations using a variety of information sources, and in doing this we are able to make decisions allowing flexibility according to need – this is especially the case in early childhood. This particular teaching skill is required by a good practitioner but tends to be either lacking or suppressed in the teacher who must stick rigidly to the syllabus which has to be followed or where examinations dominate their system.

Evaluation is intertwined with assessment and is usually defined as the judgement of performance and the appraising of situations. The two activities go hand in hand and by questioning what we are doing and how we go about it we are able to go a long way towards meeting the child's needs.

Most assessment in the form of tests happens after the learning process has taken place; this means it is of little use in deciding what the next steps should be. This is especially true when the test demonstrates previous 'disaster' and that work carried out has been to little effect. If tests are to be of real value they need to be integrated with the teaching plan and clearly relevant to the learner. Courses followed need to have tests built in at different levels and phases enabling both pupils and teachers to obtain a clear idea of the progression being achieved and providing early indications of problems. This allows teachers continually to review and refine their teaching plans in line with the needs of the pupils, and their organization to measure the effectiveness of its learning environment. It is in this way that assessment can be formative and of value in helping the child in the learning process; clearly gaps and duplications in the sequence of learning can be significantly reduced if continuous assessment techniques are an integral part of the teacher's lesson-planning processes.

TESTS AND ASSESSMENT

In order that teachers effectively use the information gained, the appropriate assessment technique must be carefully thought through and planned for in the overall teaching strategy for the subject area. Appropriate tests are common means of assessment and evaluation, but they need to be chosen with extreme care. Quite often their purpose and method of operation is not properly understood by either pupils or users.

The key questions to be answered are:

— What do we need to know from the test?
— What use are we going to make of the results?

This section is not intended to be a detailed description of the many types of test available, but a brief commentary on two of the major classes:

a) *Criteria-referenced tests*

These are useful in assessing whether particular standards or criteria have been achieved. These tests are not generally designed to measure children's abilities in relation to those of other children. Primarily they are designed to check the degree to which skills in key areas have been mastered. Most frequently they are used to determine the level of knowledge or skill before moving a child on to the next stage of learning.

b) *Norm-referenced tests*

These are tests concerned mainly with the measurement of aptitude, intelligence and personality rather than attainment. They are discriminating tests in which the performance of one pupil can be compared with the performance of a similar group of pupils.

In practice, assessment tends to involve elements of both types of test.

Recently great attention has been drawn towards 'benchmark' testing with the advent of government proposals to introduce testing for all at the ages of 7, 11 and 14 years – these could be expected to take the form of sets of criteria-referenced tests. There is considerable debate as to whether such tests, based on national requirements, benefit the pupil or satisfy parents or the needs of educational assessment and evaluation systems; such controversy is not new and will undoubtedly continue. The majority of schools

TRANSITION AND CONTINUITY

```
CURRICULUM          INITIAL         INDIVIDUAL         METHODS         RECORD
TEACHING      →    ASSESSMENT  →   TEACHING      →   ARRANGEMENT  →   KEEPING
PROGRAMMES                         PROGRAMMES
```

already use some tests, but this is usually in the context of planning the child's future progress and not for general use, particularly in the primary sector.

Records are of real benefit when they are related to defined curriculum areas and specific learning objectives and, wherever feasible, accompanied by suitable test results.

There have been considerable efforts in many schools to produce 'profile' types of records and these should not be discarded with the proposals on the National Curriculum and the need for benchmark testing, neither should they cause such existing good work to be repeated or undone. The need for records exists not only in areas such as reading development, science and mathematics, but also in other areas of the curriculum which equally need to be accurately and adequately documented.

ASSESSMENT THROUGH TEACHING

Assessment involves a variety of different techniques and, for teachers to build on these, observation of pupil performance is of vital importance.

The 'assessment through teaching' model (adapted from Delecco and Crawford, 1974 by Pearson and Lindsay in 1986) provides a useful basis for understanding the issues involved: using this type of model, assessment is seen for what it really ought to be – a continuous process using criterion-referenced measures. These authors rightly point out that 'assessment, curriculum and record keeping have become inextricably interrelated, a single integrated process'. In my experience, teachers operating this or similar models are more effective at meeting the needs of the individual pupil, but have to be sufficiently committed to the benefits and accept the demands the approach makes upon them.

The following is a quotation from the DES publication *The Curriculum 5 to 16* and refers to the Aims of Assessment as viewed by them:

> If schools are to fulfil these aims of assessment, development is needed in three main areas:

- clearer definition of expectations as expressed through the aims and objectives of curricula and schemes of work,
- improved methods of assessment in the classroom on a day-to-day basis, and
- improved methods of recording and reporting progress.

As mentioned earlier, the work by Southampton University with the Hampshire Assessment project highlights the influences that a National Curriculum and the associated bench-mark tests could have in focusing attention too narrowly on the core subjects. Teachers undoubtedly will teach according to such emphases!

As part of a national monitoring scheme, the Assessment of Performance Unit (APU) was established by the DES in the 1970s and funded to conduct surveys in curriculum areas such as mathematics, science, English and foreign languages. The aims are to discover how children of all abilities approach and perform tasks in these subjects. As a result, many new techniques of assessment have been developed and these, together with ideas on how teachers can implement them, have now been circulated to all schools. Research is still progressing aimed at studying the teaching strategies which will help pupils to avoid the most frequent misconceptions and making the more common errors.

The APU disseminates findings to improve curriculum to the previously mentioned SCDC and SEC.

TRANSFER DOCUMENTATION

What information should be available for transfer from one school to another? Clearly, the systems currently vary considerably between authorities although this could well be brought closer into line now that the GERBIL has passed into legislation. What is more important is to define the essential features of such documentation so that any interim decisions will need minimum modification in the future. This was well defined by Stillman and Maychell in 1984:

1. There should be uniformity in presentation and comparability of assessments.
2. Subject information should be needs-related, ie it should provide what the receiving school wants.
3. Information should take as direct a route as possible between the compiler(s) and user(s).
4. There should be the possibility of different types of assessment for different subject needs.

5. Information should be available when it is needed.

This is described in more detail and in priority order by Clift, Weinser and Wilson (1981):

a) Pupil's name, date of birth and home address.
b) Vital information for the child's well-being.
c) Person(s) to contact in emergency.
d) Details of any handicaps, physical or socio-emotional, which may affect school progress.
e) Details of any impediments to learning, including language.
f) Details of referrals to psychologists, reports from social workers, educational welfare officers, school medical officers, *et seq.*
g) Details of prescribed remedial treatment.
h) Stages reached in reading, language and mathematics schemes.
i) Details of any screening or other tests carried out.
j) Other medical, academic or personal information.

They did not see it as necessary to consolidate all the information on one document, providing it is readily available to those who might need to use it. Clearly, this could become less of a problem if authorities and schools were able to set up and use networked computer databases which are sufficiently secure and access-protected.

Profiling

This terminology is becoming more generally used when discussing educational measurement. With the focus constantly being on standards of performance in schools and colleges, measurement and testing need to be clearly presented to anyone with a right to require information about a particular student. Profiling is one means of presenting a collection of such information in a cohesive, relevant and meaningful way.

Undoubtedly, techniques of profiling are likely to feature increasingly in the teachers required skills in the future – the ILEA, for example, are working on producing profiling guidelines for primary children. Not only is profiling a very effective way of recording information about a pupil which can be used for continuity purposes, but many of the examination bodies are increasingly making this process a requirement of their validation criteria, CPVE for example.

WHAT IS A 'PROFILE?'

A 'profile' is fundamentally a systematic way of presenting information about a person relating to their performance, achievements and attributes.

Frith and Macintosh in 1984 stated that a profile ought to contain three basic elements:

- a list of items such as subject skills, personal qualities and course descriptions;
- means of indicating the level and/or the nature of the performance in respect of each chosen item on the list; the descriptions used can include such entries as marks, grades, subjective reports, percentages, histograms, graphs etc, but all make use of some combination of letters or numbers;
- some clear indication of the means by which the descriptions of the pupil have been arrived at.

Many profile systems in current use unfortunately neglect this last element, significantly detracting from the potential value of such profiles.

BACKGROUND TO PROFILING

A very welcome proposal from the DES in 1984 was that all young people on leaving their secondary education should take with them 'records of achievement'. This was instrumental in a major review of the records of progress which were then being compiled.

There had been a growing concern prior to that time about the very restricted nature of the 16+ and 18+ examination systems both among teachers and those who had used the results subsequently. Clearly such examination systems seldom reflected the true potential and performance capability of the pupil. With the move towards the comprehensive system of education and the growth of large-scale youth unemployment, pressure has been continually growing to focus on the assessment of all pupils and not just on those capable of academic achievement. Consequently the emphasis is to move away from mere grading and labelling towards diagnostic and evaluative approaches; at the same time, reference-based comparisons are now more frequent than the use of 'norm' criteria.

A major reason for the move towards profiling systems comes from the needs of industry and commerce to have better information on the students' mastery of skills, their attitudes and particular attributes which would make them more employable when assessing their suitability for particular demands to specific jobs.

In the section on assessment it was stated that the use of records concerning the pupil's progress were powerful tools in designing appropriate learning processes. There is no doubt that all the following can plan the educational progress of the individual child better if they have access to accurately compiled and comprehensive profile information:

— teachers, in order to plan the curriculum and manage the learning process;
— parents, in having a more complete and accurate picture of their child's progress, attainment, strengths and weaknesses;
— employers, in order that they can avoid the mutual frustrations associated with appointing unsuitable candidates;
— administrators of schemes for the unemployed, in being able to use information which can aid the selection of the most suitable training programmes.

In 1972 the Scottish School Teachers Association established a working party to review the records produced for those who left school without obtaining any of the nationally recognized certificates. (The report was called *Pupils in Profile,* 1977.) The essentials of their assessment scheme were based on a cumulative assessment document which was open to both pupils and their parents to read at all stages. This scheme was modified considerably before being adopted nationally in Scotland and it was certainly instrumental in alerting the attention of those in England and Wales.

Throughout the UK there is now tremendous enthusiasm about the development of profiling systems for recording children's progress and this is permeating through all stages of development, not just at the very early and later educational mileposts as was formerly the case. This enthusiasm has fostered a growing body of experience and expertise.

CURRENT APPROACHES
In order that good practices could be shared with the results of pilot projects, there was a need for a more formal network to be formed. The Dorset Educational Authority and the Southern Examinations Board in 1984 established a research and development project called the National Profiling Network to meet this

SPECIFIC TECHNIQUES

need. The aims of this network are to offer services to participants, such as:

- a list of practitioners with details of their work, which is regularly updated;
- a catalogue of publications relating to profile assessment and records of achievement, again regularly updated;
- a central 'postbox' for the dissemination of work;
- a regular newsletter dealing with current issues;
- appropriate conference services;
- publication of a series of discussion papers focusing attention on major curriculum and assessment issues.

Initially this network was financed by the originator, but it is now available to annual corporate and individual membership subscription and is of considerable value to practitioners in aiding their development work. Sharing experience and expertise in this way can only enhance the effective provision of accurate records to accompany children throughout their education.

The difficulty with a personalized profile record system is how to give it national recognition and accreditation. There is considerable variation in format, content and titles used. Many systems have been developed within an authority or a particular school or by a group of neighbouring schools for their own particular purposes. The government recognized this rapid proliferation in the development of record keeping systems and issued a draft policy in 1983, which gained much support, aimed at introducing records of achievement. A further statement was issued in 1984 which determined the way in which a national system for agreeing and establishing records of achievement could take place. The target date for the completion of this exercise is 1990 for all school-leavers in England and Wales. The government followed this up with nine pilot schemes to gain a wider band of exposure and experience; these were funded by Educational Support Grants to work for three years from April 1985. The steering committee for this initiative is scheduled to report in autumn 1988 on the experiences gained and is expected to recommend national guidelines from which a recognized system for records of achievement can be established.

The DES sent a copy of the government's booklet on *Records of Achievement – A Statement of Policy* in 1986 to all schools. This carried information on all of the pilot schemes in which contacts could be made. The Hampshire LEA, concerned with their continuing review of record keeping and assessment, set up their own (Primary Schools Pupil Assessment) project in conjunction with the Assessment and Examinations unit of Southampton University, with the focus on inter-school transfer in 1986. The school pyramid concept was used, as in other LEAs, for meetings and visits between primary and secondary teaching staffs. The main issues studied were the pupil transfer records, continuity of the curriculum, pyramid initiatives and pupil induction into the secondary environment. These are all areas which must raise relevant questions to others embarking on an investigation of practices in similar arenas.

Conclusions concerning profiling

The advantages of a profiling system to maintain records have been outlined already, but the real gains of such an approach are made if the pupil and parents are kept involved throughout the compilation processes. If nothing more, this minimizes the risk of them receiving unpleasant shocks at the end of an educational stage, when it is too late to really recover the situation or take a more appropriate course of action. It is the partnership between parent and teacher that must be strived for if mutual trust and understanding are to prevail and be of benefit to the child; this can only result from the sharing of a continuous record of performance.

Greater emphasis, undoubtedly, will be placed on 'assessment over time', upon observation and a higher degree of informality. This inevitably places extra demands on teachers, who must be ready to undertake training in the construction and use of profiles if they are to be effective. There will also be a need to make time to complete the documentation required; initially this may well seem an extra burden, but as time passes and the system becomes part of the standard procedures for teachers, the advantages will far outweigh the administrative effort needed.

At present there are discontinuities in ongoing/formative and terminal/summative uses of assessment and in the credibility of profiles currently being used.

> There are problems associated with measurement and the presentation of information about personal qualities, problems associated with the measurement and presentation of information regarding progress over time, and finally, the implications of a negotiated curriculum for its evaluation and for the assessment of individuals ... (Frith and Macintosh, 1984)

In view of the latest set of governmental proposals to introduce a national arrangement for records of achievement for all by 1990, many of these discontinuities should disappear. Profiles certainly offer a far more detailed and comprehensive account of the achievements of school-leavers than was previously feasible. They can be designed to contain details of extra-curricular and out-of-school achievements in addition to information relating to personal qualities. Without any doubt, profile systems probably offer the most comprehensive and potentially useful set of information criteria for pupil, teacher and parents as well as being more meaningful and relevant to the needs of employers.

RECORDS OF ACHIEVEMENT

Consortia set up as pilot groups and funded through the TVEI Programme are examining the use of profiles and records of achievement for school-leavers; these consortia include both employers and lecturing staff from colleges of FE.

In 1984 the government issued a policy statement on profiling and records of achievement, recommending that young people leaving schools or colleges should take with them a short summary document of their records which is recognized and valued by employers and FE establishments. This was expected to provide a more rounded picture of candidates for jobs or courses (both academic and vocational) than could be provided by a list of exam reports or a final school 'reference'. The belief was that such a document would enable potential users to decide better how the leaver could be suitably employed or matched to appropriate training schemes or further study. This was a greater move towards continuity at this stage of the educational process than had previously been made, particularly as it was proposed that not only was curriculum performance and potential to be recorded, but also a note made of the person's 'motivation and personal development'.

In 1987 an interim report was produced on *Records of Achievement* by the National Steering Committee. This made clear the committee's belief that the educational philosophy which these records of achievement are helping teachers to develop are consistent with that required for establishing the National Curriculum. It states:

> The work which teachers have been pioneering on records of achievement, the discussion with pupils about their progress and responsibility for their own learning, the regular and systematic recording of

educational progress and the presentation of information about achievement in a short and succinct form for parents and employers – all these will be of immediate relevance to schools in introducing the National Curriculum. (DES, 1987 *Records of Achievement*).

It is anticipated that all schools should have such summary documents available by 1995.

It is encouraging that pupils and parents are to be involved and consulted throughout, but a lot of resources need to be made available for this to be a practical and effective proposition. The aim is for the teacher to have sufficient time to record, review and discuss the entries with pupils and parents. Teachers will need to be adequately prepared for these activities – new teachers during their basic certification and existing ones through in-service programmes. This cannot be left to chance if this system of recording achievement is to produce consistent and usable results nationally.

Curriculum structure

To attempt to cover the subject of curriculum structure in this book would be an impossible task; so much has been written on it. It is possible, however, to highlight the fact that a clearly defined thread should run through the educational process.

Many demands are made on the curriculum at various times and, for a variety of reasons, cause it to change, but there should always be a unity of purpose throughout so that the pupil does not encounter radical changes of direction.

We can only start with the child and wherever they enter the educational system we must set the goals, in the words of Warnock at an educational forum in 1978, so as:

> ... to first enlarge the child's knowledge, experience and imaginative understanding and thus the awareness of moral values and capacity for enjoyment and, secondly, to enable the child to enter the world after formal education is over as an active participant in society and as a responsible contributor to it, capable of achieving as much independence as possible.

The choices offered can vary a great deal according to the autonomy of the institution, particularly when, as has been stated elsewhere, crossing from one phase to another. The major issues inevitably occur, under current practices, with the transition from primary to secondary stages. The strong child-centred approaches to curriculum contrast most severely at this point with the traditional subject-based approaches appearing necessary to the secondary system. This phenomenon is increasingly being recognized and major developments are taking place towards a cross-curricular approach in the first years of secondary schooling.

Frequently overlooked are the radical differences in the teaching traditions, attitudes and styles of each sector of education. These tend to be most noticeable when primary, secondary and further educational organizations are compared as to how they offer the curriculum to those in their care. However, more and more teachers are becoming aware of this problem and are moving towards suitable compromises which take into account the need for educational effectiveness yet allow for economic efficiency. This is particularly noticeable with teaching structures which are based on integrated CDT curricula and TVEI where particular pressures now exist for co-ordination of the continuity necessary between secondary and further educational syllabi. It would not be desirable, however, to move away completely from the autonomy in what is taught and of teaching styles to a totally prescribed approach; these are the very factors in our system, despite all its faults, which are the envy of many other parts of the world, in particular of European countries. A national curiculum would certainly bring about uniformity and equal opportunity regarding what is on offer, providing that there is a built-in flexibility to:

a) cater for local or special needs and
b) implement the curriculum according to the needs of the pupils.

The thread of continuity which is essential is in building on what has gone before and preparing for what will be undertaken subsequently. The curriculum guidelines formulated by the LEAs in response to the White Paper (*A View of the Curriculum*) 6/81 can only have helped continuity in education for children from the ages of 3 to 16 years.

Development planning

Further aid to continuity for pupils in the educational process has arisen from the concepts now adopted by many local authorities for the production of 'school development plans' and the formation of clusters and networks of schools. In some cases this clustering type of arrangement is extended into further education, particularly where colleges running on tertiary lines exist.

Originally established in the ILEA, 'clusters' were formed incorporating secondary schools and their feeder schools to liaise and perhaps look at joint in-service training needs, with the main objective being the improvement of the pupil's learning opportunities. In a similar fashion the 'pyramids', mentioned in the section on profiling, have been established by other LEAs to encourage planned continuity between establishments.

School development plans are a means of enabling the school to assess its current position and consider its curriculum planning and resourcing in the light of stated future objectives. By carefully planning actions and determining target dates the school can then focus on its key priorities, which then permits proper monitoring of achievement and progress. Schools must be accountable for their own actions and such methods permit them to present evidence of their growth, yet be in control of their own planning processes within the governmental or local authority policies. Ideally, and where it is already occurring, the plan will be developed with the involvement of others who can provide a meaningful contribution, such as governors, parents and the LEA. This process can only be seen as a positive move towards the goverment's aims in the 1988 Education Reform Act which specifically requires much greater involvement of both parent and governors in the running of their schools.

CHAPTER 8

A SUMMARY AND OVERVIEW OF THE CURRENT SITUATION

In conclusion, after what has been a look into the many practices in crossing the various bridges in transition, it is encouraging to note how much more awareness has been awakened recently in the need to understand the discontinuities which can occur.

In early years, leaving home and starting school is often considered a priority area and schools and nurseries are devoting more time and effort to smoothing that pathway. Teachers, with the help of parents, are giving more time to home visiting and children and parents spend more time prior to entry helping the child to become familiar with and feel secure in the new environment. More teachers are becoming aware of the need to start with 'where the child is' in the stage of development and build on the experience that has already been established.

Transition and continuity practices from infant to junior and, particularly, from junior to secondary, is growing rapidly with the financial impetus that has been gained from the better in-service provisions resulting from the most recent (1987) Local Education Authority Grant Training Scheme. Teachers can easily be given more time (with supply teacher cover) to form joint 'workshops' with other classes to work on curriculum documentation and arrange joint staff meetings around selected topic areas. This can only aid curriculum continuity and the implementation of a National Curriculum should ensure more uniformity and consensus across the primary feeder schools. The only proviso is that there will need to be sufficient flexibility in the curriculum laid down to allow for the opportunities which can be built into the broad range of options currently available. The Hampshire primary pupil assessment programme – that was set up in 1986 and has contributed greatly to advancing methods of inter-school transfer and the valuable work they continue to do – works jointly with the assessment and examinations unit at Southampton University towards curriculum continuity through pupil transfer records, pyramid structures and pupil induction into secondary schools. The pyramid concept piloted in Hampshire and Dorset and other authorities is a great step forward in promoting good continuity for pupils across the various bridges of transition.

As already discussed, there has also been considerable progress in liaison and there is growing concern for continuity at the post-16 stages, some of this as response to other initiatives such as TVEI; schools, colleges and potential employers are becoming increasingly involved in planning for continuity into the workplace. Community involvement is invaluable and there is a need to continue to seek ways to ensure that this involvement grows. Education is not just confined to schools, it is also the responsibility of parents and the community in partnership. The emphasis on parental involvement at all levels cannot be too strongly stressed. It is the major influence on children's attitude towards learning and their motivation to make the most of their educational opportunities. The reason why many children become 'switched off' is because of the wrong 'messages' or disinterest shown by adults and, in particular, their parents' attitudes. Teachers must understand how to develop relationships with parents to help them feel confident with the major contributions they can make towards their children's education. To do this they need to recognize and develop a set of social skills which will enable them to accomplish this. More must be done to include parents and create a continuing interest in their child's journey through the educational process.

What are the major discontinuities which need the most urgent attention? There are three parties fundamentally involved: national and local government; headteachers and their heads of departmental activities; and, most important of all, the class teachers themselves. While policies and procedures need attention, particularly at central levels, it must have become clear through the examples given in this book how much can be achieved by the well-informed teacher who has the support of the headteacher.

More priority in the form of national commitment and LEA resourcing needs to be given to this area. The long-term benefit both nationally and locally is obvious, in particular in minimizing the costly remedial actions which arise from early discontinuities in a pupil's education. The Education Reform Act (1988) proposes some major changes – such as a National Curriculum, open enrolment, testing and direct control – all of which could be divisive and thus it is uncertain how they may affect continuity, but I anticipate that it should enhance rather than hinder continuity across phases. These changes are wide-ranging and the effects of some of the proposals are already beginning to affect educational planning, such as those discussed below.

a) The previously mentioned National Curriculum proposals should help, but will control of its content be retained entirely at central government level? The rhetoric of the current government has always stressed the need to devolve more power to governing bodies and parents!
b) Certainly, open enrolment suggests that parents will have unlimited choice and queues are likely to form at the popular schools. This could create havoc across phases where schools will no longer have recognized catchment areas; this could be a particular problem in the larger urban and city conurbations where the logistics of transport make a wide variety of choice a real possibility.
c) Opting out will require very careful consideration and, for many, a requirement to learn a whole new range of skills in resource management which have previously been the responsibility of the LEA. If they take this route schools and colleges will have to plan and administer resources and face up to the often conflicting, educational, political and parental demands and priorities which arise when decisions on how resources are to be allocated are taken. Governing bodies will require very skilled and educationally knowledgeable members if they are to take responsibility for financial management, decisions on curriculum continuity and content, staff appointments, selection of teaching materials, etc. It must also be remembered that these people will at the same time be giving their services voluntarily and will need to devote considerable time to the transitional process.
d) Possibly the most emotive issue is that of the national testing proposal at ages 7, 11 and 14 years for all children. The main objections are that it could label young children and result in inappropriate comparisons with children from the same school or other schools. I think we should reserve judgement until we have the final structure of the system.

The initiatives in this Reform Act will certainly be felt quickly but the results will take several years. Nevertheless, if properly administered there is very good scope for improved educational transition and continuity.

An important feature in curriculum continuity is the pressure on teachers and resources. One element which is not given sufficient emphasis is the continual need to review the teaching styles and methods adopted by teachers throughout both primary and secondary education. These can be major causes of discontinuity and yet they are not even considered in the current government proposals. Looking at the pressures on teachers, particularly in the secondary sector, it is worth reflecting on the many changes which they have had to accommodate over recent years, for example:

— the implications of the Warnock report in the 1981 Education Act;
— the introduction of TVEI;
— the introduction of CPVE;
— the need for records of achievement and profiling;
— the introduction of GCSE; and
— the introduction of the National Curriculum, and testing.

Insufficient thought has so often preceded these changes in curriculum and practice as to how they should be resourced and staffed, both in terms of the materials and the time needed. The introduction of the GCSE is a classic example even allowing for the disruptions of the teachers' dispute. Such changes have often been too rapid with no time to reflect and evaluate the changes of methodology required from those who have the real job of implementation – the class teacher. The national shortage in recruitment of secondary teachers must partly be a result of this.

Other discontinuities at the primary to secondary transfer stage must be the result of geographical and to some extent parental choice, where some secondary schools receive pupils from a very wide range of primary schools with occasionally only one or two children from some of these; in such cases it is a mammoth task to create effective systems to ensure good liaison and continuity. The situation is not made any easier where some primary schools are sending children on to seven or eight secondary schools or to independent schools in certain areas.

When the DES and LEAs design in-service training programmes and approve teacher training curricula, it is essential that there is representation across all phases at some point in order that implications and factors affecting educational transition and continuity are properly taken into account. More training needs to be made available regarding the specific purpose of fostering good practices in continuity and transition, particularly between the sectors.

There is much to do, but we must continue to strive towards the overriding goal of 'continuity in the curriculum' for all children to help them across the many bridges they will encounter.

References

Bate, Hargreaves and Gibson (1982) *Experimental Liaison Groups in Early Education* The Schools Council
Bennett, Desforges, Cockburn and Wilson (1984) *The Quality of Pupils' Learning Experiences* Lawrence Erlbaum Associates
Benyon, Lois (1984) *Curriculum* vol 5 no 1
Blatchford, P (1979) *The Development of Social Interaction Between Infants*
Blatchford, Battle and Mays (1982) *The First Transition* NFER-Nelson, Windsor
Bloom, Benjamin (1964) *Stability and Change in the Human Character* Wiley, New York
Bowlby, J (1971) *Attachment and Loss* Vol 1 Penguin
British Association for Early Childhood Education (1984) unpublished internal report
Bruner, J S (1975) *Entry into Early Language – A Spiral Curriculum* 1st edn 1960. University of Swansea
Bruner, J S (1977) *The Process of Education* Harvard University Press, Cambridge, Massachusetts
Bruner, J S et al (1980) *The Oxford Pre-school Research Project* Grant McIntyre
Bruner, J S (1980) *Under 5s in Britain* Grant McIntyre
Cleave, S, Jowett and Bate, M (1982) *And So to School* NFER-Nelson, Windsor
Clift, P, Weiner, G, and Wilson, E (1981) *Record-keeping in Primary Schools* Macmillan Educational
The Council of Europe (1985) *The Link Between Pre-school and Primary Education* (Symposium report), Versailles
Crowe, B (1973) *The Playgroup Movement* Unwin
Curtis, A (1986) *A Curriculum for the Pre-school Child* NFER Nelson, Windsor
Dean, J (1985) Continuity of education *in* Richards, C (ed) *A Study of Primary Education* Falmer Press, Lewes
Department of Education and Science (1975) (circular) Special Education from Health to Education, HMSO
Department of Education and Science (1978) *The Primary Report – Primary Education in England* HMSO

REFERENCES

Department of Education and Science (1980) *A View of the Curriculum* HMSO

Department of Education and Science (1981) *The Practical Curriculum* HMSO

Department of Education and Science (1982) *Education 5–9. The First School Report* HMSO

Department of Education and Science (1981) (circular) The School Curriculum, HMSO

Department of Education and Science (1985) *The Curriculum 5–16* HMSO

Department of Education and Science (1987) *Records of Achievement* Report of Records of Achievement National Steering Committee. HMSO

Department of Education and Science (1987) (circular) Local Education Authority Training Grants Scheme: Financial Year 1988/9, HMSO

Department of Education and Science(1987) (circular) Approval for Courses of Further Training for School and Further Education Teachers in England 1988/9, HMSO

Delecco, J R and Crawford, W R (1967) *The Psychology of Language, Thought and Instruction*

Dewey, J (1938) *Experiences in Education* Macmillan

De Witt (1977) Links between pre-school and primary education, part 2, the establishment of continuity. A conference document, Bournemouth

Frith and Macintosh (1984) *A Teacher's Guide to Assessment* Stanley Thornes

Findlay (1985) *Education 3-13,* vol 11 no 1, Falmer Press

The Fish Report (1985) *Educational Opportunities for All* Inner London Education Authority

Hadow (1926) *The Hadow Report on Secondary Education* Department of Education

Hadow (1931) *The Hadow Report on Primary Education* Depart of Education

Hargreaves, D (1985) *Improving Secondary Schools* ILEA

Jennings, K and Hargreaves, D (1977) Children's attitudes to secondary school transfer *in Educational Studies* vol **7** no 1

Marland, M (1977) *Language Across the Curriculum* Heinemann

Mayell, B and Petrie, P (1977) *Mother, Minder and Child* University of London Institute of Education

Measor and Woods (1984) *Changing Schools* Oxford University Press

National Foundation for Educational Research (1978) Unpublished document on record keeping

Pearson and Lindsay (1986) *Special Needs in the Primary Classroom* NFER-Nelson

Piaget, J (1954) *Origins of Intelligence* Basic Books, New York

Piaget, J (1961) *The Growth of Understanding in the Young Child* Educational Supply Association

Piaget, J and Inhelder (1969) *The Psychology of the Child* Routledge and Kegan Paul

The Plowden Report (1967) *Children and their Primary Schools* HMSO

Roberts, M (1981) *Early Childhood*
Scottish Council for Research in Education (1977) *Pupils in Profile* Report
Shipman, M (1983) *Assessment in Primary amd Middle Schools* Teaching 5-13 Series. Croom Helm
Spens (1938) *The Spens Report on Secondary Education* Department of Education and Science, The Consultative Committee
Stillman and Maychell (1984) *School to School* NFER-Nelson
Straker-Welds (1984) *Education for a Multi-cultural Society* Bell and Hyman
Sylva, K and Lunt, I (1982) *Child Development; a First Course* Basil Blackwell
The Thomas Report (1985) *Improving Primary Schools* Inner London Education Authority
Times Educational Supplement February, 1976
Tizard, Mortimer and Burchell (1981) *Involving Parents in Nursery and Infant Schools* Grant McIntyre
Tizard and Hughes (1984) *Young Children Learning* Fontana
Walkerdine (1982) *Personal Communication*
Warnock (1978) *The Warnock Report: The Education of Handicapped Children and Young Persons* DES
Watt, J (1985) *The Role of Parents in the Continuity of Children's Education*
Wells, C (1985) *Language Development in the Pre-school Years* Cambridge University Press
Woodhead, M (1985) *Oxford Review of Education*
Youngman, M B (1980) Some determinants of early secondary school performance *in British Journal of Educational Psychology* no 50